AF506015

Modern American Reading Practices

MODERN AMERICAN READING PRACTICES

BETWEEN AESTHETICS AND HISTORY

Philip Goldstein

Contents

CONTENTS

ACKNOWLEDGMENTS

I am grateful to the University of Delaware for the leave and to Columbia University for the facilities that enabled me to write this book. I thank my wife Leslie for her constant support, and Jim Machor, Carsten Strathausen, and other friends at the Marxist Literary Group and the Reception Study Society for their interest in my work. I also thank Oxford University Press for permission to reprint "Richard Wright's *Native Son*: From Naturalist Protest to Modernist Liberation and Beyond" (*New Directions in Reception Study*, ed. P. Goldstein and J. Machor [Oxford: Oxford UP, 2008], 119–36), which forms Chapter 5, and *The Reader* for permission to reprint "The Politics of Sara Paretsky's Detective Fiction" (*The Reader* 55 [Fall 2006]), which forms Chapter 7.

MODERN AMERICAN READING PRACTICES

BETWEEN AESTHETICS AND HISTORY

> What I have been saying is that, whatever they do, it will only be interpretation in another guise because, like it or not, interpretation is the only game in town.
>
> Stanley Fish, *Is There a Text in This Class?*

IN "LEARNING HOW TO READ SLOWLY AGAIN," Williams Grimes commends Francine Prose's *Reading Like A Writer* because it gets "the electricity flowing the right way again" by "zeroing in on single words, then sentences, then paragraphs, teasing out the specifics that transmute raw language into style and an artistically meaningful form." Similarly, Edward Mendelson's *Things That Matter* "gets right down," Grimes says, "to the heavy work of close reading" and comes up with "riches." To this list Grimes could easily have added Harold Bloom's *How to Read and Why* (2001), Thomas Foster's *How to Read Literature Like a Professor* (2003), John Sutherland's *How to Read a Novel (2006)*, and many similar books. These normative accounts of reading have grown explosively since the 1990s, when various critics dismissed the theoretical and cultural methods of the 1970s and 1980s and celebrated the pleasures of close reading or the value of aesthetic ideals.[1]

Such normative accounts are justified by these celebrations, which preserve the textual analysis that the American New Criticism and other formal approaches initiated in the 1930s and 1940s but, unhappy with their neutral objectivity, emphasize reading's pleasures, which can, they claim, rejuvenate the study of literature. This unhappiness moved Denis Donaghue, for example, to adopt what he calls "aesthetic reading," in which the critic or student engages in slow, careful reading and experiences its resulting delights and imaginative freedom (*Reading* 12–13, 56, 73). Similarly, in *Required Reading*, Andrew Delbanco complains that, instead of introducing students of literature to the "experience of intense delight" (214), literary critics have turned texts into "excretions through which, while holding our noses, we search for traces of the maladies of our culture."

Other critics defend the subversive force of aesthetic ideals rather than the delights of careful reading. Some of these critics claim that Theodor Adorno's Marxist aesthetics has grown more important since the 1990s because, as I explain in Chapter 1, the close reading that it fosters reveals the implicit contradictions of the capitalist social order and rejects, thereby, the identity politics of feminist, black, or postcolonial scholars and the textual or linguistic critiques of Derridean or poststructuralist scholars.[2] Other scholars argue that, on the contrary, it is those who deny the subversive negativity of aesthetics who promote radical and Marxist views, employ reductive political or ideological criteria, and ensure literature's marginal status.[3]

These critics defend the pleasures of reading or the autonomy and negativity of aesthetic ideals and justify normative accounts of reading. Other critics, by contrast, reject such aesthetic autonomy or close textual analysis on the grounds that aesthetic ideals reflect the interpreter's psychological or sociohistorical context rather than an autonomous norm. Reader-response critics argue, for example, that reading projects the identity of the reader or the critic onto the text. As David Bleich says, the text's aesthetics "do not matter" ("Literature" 309) because interpretation invariably reveals the personality of the reader.[4] Sociological critics also maintain that aesthetics do not matter, but they argue that the class background or social context of the reader, not the personality, explains his or her responses.[5]

More sharply than in previous eras, critics defend sociohistorical accounts of a text against normative, aesthetic accounts, or, conversely, the aesthetics of the text against political or historical accounts of it. Of course, such disputes are nothing new. They began when Aristotle argued that in a tragedy the fall of a hero nobler than the spectators evokes their pity and fear. In the early twenty-first century such disputes have acquired a new impetus because literary study now includes a broad array of reading practices. Interpretation is, as Stanley Fish says, "the only game in town," because these reading practices may now include, in addition to the traditional intention of the author, the reader's reactions; the text's figures, structure, or rhetoric; various media, including television, movies, magazines, and newspapers; as well as the sexuality, gender, race, or nationality of the author, reader, media, or text. This explosion of reading practices has intensified the opposition of normative aesthetic approaches and reader response, social, historical, and cultural approaches; however, as I will show, the historical study of reading practices moves beyond opposition. Unlike the aesthetic approaches, which repudiate the political or social influences on reading and defend the autonomy of aesthetic ideals, and the reader-response, historical, or cultural approaches, which repudiate their autonomy and examine their psychological or sociohistorical determination, the historical study of reading practices grants the limited aesthetic autonomy of these practices and reveals their changing historical contexts.

READING PRACTICES

This historical study examines the cultural, theoretical, or sociohistorical grounds of the reader's interpretations but does not repudiate the aesthetic import of interpretive practices or preserve the absolute autonomy of aesthetic norms or the individual pleasures of reading; rather, this study grants aesthetics autonomy within its diverse textual, social, or cultural contexts. This approach assumes, in other words, that, far from a blank slate, a text comes to readers already constructed by editors, schools, movies, friends, family, and commentary. For instance, the modern versions of *Hamlet* are compiled from a folio and two quarto versions, which were produced at different times, differ greatly in substance, and reflect different editorial theories. Some scholars have suggested that the first quarto may be a legitimate, early version of the play and that, revised by Shakespeare and his company, the second quarto may have provided the working text for the first folio (Jones 76; Urkowitz 259–66; Werstine 81). Other scholars dismiss the first quarto, which J. Dover Wilson calls a "ridiculous text" reconstructed by a "wild ass" (xiii, 20), and try to reconstruct an original or, as Wilson says, autograph version of the play. These contrary theories inform the editions of the play, which include a version presenting all three texts simultaneously so as to allow the reader to construct the best text.

In addition to the various editions, the play's many interpretations also reveal theoretical grounding that produce contrary versions of the play. For example, in one well-known account, Hamlet plans to avenge his father's murder but, because of his speculative mind, his melancholy nature, or his mother's unseemly sexual appetite, neglects the revenge until the end, when not only Claudius but Hamlet and many others die. Urged by the ghost to revenge his "most foul and unnatural murder," Hamlet vows to remember him, notes in his "tables . . . That one may smile, and smile, and be a villain" (1, 2, 108), but, instead of taking any action, lapses into what he terms an "antic disposition" or laments that he "must, like a whore, unpack his heart with words" Only during his last moments does he finally take revenge, killing Claudius with both the poisoned wine and the sword and urging Horatio to live on to tell his story. According to other accounts, the text shows the contrary view: a man of action, he takes revenge from the start, not just at the end. As he says after he sees the ghost, "The time is out of joint. O Cursèd spite, That ever I was born to set it right!" (I, 5, 188-89). In other words, the text shows both that from the start Hamlet takes revenge, engaging in idealist reforms whose failure leaves him no option but to kill Claudius, and that, until the end, Hamlet engages in philosophical speculations that put off or neglect the revenge until the very end. Before I explain what makes these contrary readings possible, I should note that these readings adopt the Aristotelian assumption that in a tragedy the superior hero reveals a flaw and, as a result, suffers a fall filling the spectators with pity and fear. What unifies the play but undermines these generic features are, as other readings suggest, its symbols of death and decay. Although the play reasserts its dramatic form, especially at the end, when Hamlet kills Claudius with the sword and his "union," the images and metaphors of loss, decay, and death unify the play, rendering it independent of its tragic form. I could go on to argue that the antithetical metaphors or historical connotations of the text's language undermine both the tragic form and the unifying images of the play, but I have said enough to suggest that the play presents contradictory versions of itself. It is a tragedy in which Hamlet takes action from the start, demanding reforms whose failures he does not recognize until the end, as well as a tragedy in which, because of his extensive speculations, his melancholy nature, or his mother's unseemly sexual appetite, Hamlet grows too depressed to do anything until the very end. The play is also a symbolic entity unified by its images of loss, decay, and death, not its tragic form, as well as a mode of historical or rhetorical discourse undermining this unity and form.

Critics who consider the play a tragedy in which Hamlet takes action from the start maintain that it depicts the dilemmas of the Renaissance as well as the modern intellectual idealist, who, upset by Gertrude's "o'erhasty" marriage and the ghost's disturbing revelations, discovers that a shocking corruption and brutal inhumanity pervade Danish society and tries but fails to reform it (see Kiernan 68; Kettle 238; Kernan, *Magician* 93; Margolies 66–67; Siegel). This account justifies neoclassical humanism, which originated in the Renaissance and which in its Marxist versions defends the unified human self against the fragmentation imposed by sociohistorical change, commodity production, disciplinary divisions, etc.

Other critics, who include Samuel T. Coleridge, A. C. Bradley, Earnest Jones, and Janet Adelman, adopt the view that the play depicts a Hamlet who, because of his extensive speculations, his melancholy nature, or his mother's unseemly sexual appetite, grows too depressed to do anything. This version began in the Romantic era when, to defend middle-class English literature against the aristocratic classical tradition, critics construed the play as the overflowing expression of Shakespeare's genius. In the Victorian and early modern era, when criticism entered the university and assimilated the classical tradition, scholars such as A. C. Bradley adopted this romantic view as well as the neoclassical tragic view, construing Hamlet as a tragic hero whose melancholy state keeps him from taking action. This account made the play accessible to the nineteenth century's new middle-class reading public.

Still other critics accept this romantic or the neoclassical account but attribute Hamlet's failure to act to historical conditions, including the religious beliefs of the Elizabethans, the conventions of revenge tragedy, or the ideals of Senecan stoicism, not the evils of nascent Renaissance capitalism nor the indecision of the analytical intellectual (see Empson, Greenblatt, *Hamlet*, Levin, and Tennenhouse). Initially adopted by philological scholars, this historical method developed out of the nineteenth century's Higher Criticism of the Bible and effectively opposed absolutist or allegorical theology, which interpreted not only the Bible but classical texts as prefiguring modern religious views (see Compagnon 58–62). In the late nineteenth century, when Anglo-American universities established departments of languages and literature, the historical method was adopted by the scientific philologists and provided causal analyses of a work's sources and influences, an author's development, or an era's styles.

Other critics adopt the view that the play is unified by its images of loss, decay, and death, not its tragic form (see, for example, Knight and Clemen). Critics who accept this version deny that Hamlet takes meaningful action, occupies a world of his own, or experiences a disabling disgust with life, because it is the play's images of poison, disease, corruption, and death, not the character of Hamlet nor the pursuit of revenge, which unify the play. What authorizes this version is the formal method, which was established by the specialized scholars and independent professional associations developed in the mid-twentieth century and which opposes the historical, humanist, and romantic versions on the grounds that they adopt extrinsic sociological, psychological, or philosophical concerns rather than the images, symbols, metaphors, and other figural devices intrinsic to the play itself.

Still other scholars also deny that Hamlet takes meaningful action, experiences a disabling melancholy, or engages in speculative practices but go on to show that, far from unifying the play, its figural devices undermine the language's literal import, the text's unity, the play's generic conventions, and even the traditional critics' methodology (see Fergusson, Garber, and Hawks). What justifies these versions are Derridean or New Historical methods, which reveal the underlying layers and tensions of textual languages or the congruent character of historical and textual discourses and which both reconcile and move beyond the formal, historical, and neoclassical approaches.

Theatrical productions and movie versions also reveal theoretical assumptions, but I have said enough to suggest that neoclassical, humanist, romantic, formal, historical, Derridean, New Historical, and other approaches explain the play's contrary versions of itself. In other words, the contrary accounts of the text have emerged as those methods evolved in keeping with the changing historical contexts of readers and reading. These versions suggest, moreover, that close reading or aesthetic norms matter but involve more than the empirical analysis of the text. The sociohistorical context of the reader also matters, but aesthetic norms do not simply reflect them; rather, they justify and regulate the reader's activity and oppose contrary norms. As Tony Bennett says, "The literary text has no single or uniquely privileged meaning . . . that can be abstracted from the ways in which criticism itself works upon and mediates the reception of the text" (*Formalism* 137).

Like *Hamlet*, canonical and noncanonical British and American works, including *Frankenstein, Beloved, Absalom, Absalom!*, Sara Paretsky's detective fiction, *Native Son, Light in August, Jazz*, and *The Adventures of Huckleberry Finn*, reveal diverse or contrary versions showing "the ways in which criticism itself works upon and mediates the reception of the text." What works upon and mediates the contrary versions of those texts are, in particular, the American reader's changing cultural traditions and institutional contexts, which since WWII include the growth of women's, black, ethnic, and other programs and movements; the emergence of college educated, women, and minority readers; the increased cultural influence of universities and the media; and the sciences' domination of educational institutions. Because of these and other changes, conventional generic types and categories, including those of popular mysteries, science fiction, and realist, naturalist, modernist, and postmodernist fiction, have broken down, as has the equally conventional distinction between the public and the private realm. As a result, modern American accounts of realist, naturalist, modernist, and postmodernist art assimilate the conventions of popular mysteries, romances, science fiction, and so on, suggesting hybrid aesthetic constructs that violate traditional divisions between popular public or mass culture and private or high art. In other words, modern American reading practices do not reduce to their social, political, or cultural contexts or impose universal aesthetic norms; they foster the feminist, African American, humanist, or cultural programs and movements which promote them.

CHAPTER SUMMARIES

The first chapter of this book maintains that the historical method of Michel Foucault explains and justifies this account of modern American reading practices. This chapter argues that, unlike Adorno's aesthetics, which considers only high art and speculative theory subversive, Foucault's method makes possible cultural histories revealing the local contexts or politics of reading practices. In important ways Adorno's notion of instrumental reason and Foucault's concept of "power/knowledge" or "governmentality" parallel Martin Heidegger's and Jacques Derrida's notions of onto-theology, which describes the customs, practices, or "being" characterizing social life; however, Adorno's speculative Hegelian critique reduces these customs, traditions, practices, or "technology" to repressive political domination and grants subversive force only to speculative theory or high art. Foucault rejects, by contrast, the instrumental reason of Adorno and the equipmental reason or onto-theology of both Heidegger and Jacques Derrida and describes the positive import and historical development of those practices or technologies.

Chapter 2 explains what Foucault's methods say about reading or interpretation. For the most part, reception theorists, who include Tony Bennett, Stanley Fish, John Frow, Wolfgang Iser, Hans Robert Jauss, Stephen Mailloux, Pierre Macherey, and others, agree that readers construct the text in keeping with their aesthetic ideals and cultural values. Like Adorno and Heidegger, Wolfgang Iser and Hans Robert Jauss maintain, however, that great art moves the reader to set aside his or her preconceptions and produce a disturbing interpretation that exposes the empty conformity of modern social life. Critics of all sorts have commended this view, yet it, like Adorno's or Heidegger's account, erases the institutional contexts of literary study, including its established canons of great works, its schools of interpretation, and its place in a school's curriculum or a country's theaters, museums, libraries, or cultural offices. By contrast, the neopragmatists Stanley Fish and Stephen Mailloux and the post-Marxists Tony Bennett, John Frow, and Pierre Macherey reject the theoretical critique of Heidegger or Adorno in favor of a Foucauldian history of cultural regimes, formations, rhetorics, or interpretive communities explaining what enables the reader to produce and justify interpretations. The neopragmatist account, however, remains a speculative construct, whereas the post-Marxist account examines the history of the established cultural practices governing a reader's activity.

The remaining chapters show how readings of canonical and noncanonical Anglo-American texts have been affected by particular institutional changes. Chapter 3, for example, indicates that the aesthetic status of Mary Shelly's *Frankenstein* has changed drastically since the 1960s. For over 150 years, critics considered *Frankenstein* an improbable, immoral, disunified story with a didactic style and heretical views and Mary Shelley an uncreative writer, an irresponsible mother, and a clinging, sycophantic wife. Since the 1960s, critics have found Mary Shelley original, insightful, and critical and the novel, rich, meaningful, and irreducible, what George Levine and U. C. Knoepflmacher term, in the anthology that began the new appreciation of the novel, "both inexhaustible and inexplicable." I do not mean to deny that the formal devices, moral truth, social criticism, or aesthetic irreducibility that scholars now attribute to these novels justify their revaluation; I mean to suggest that nineteenth-century critics devalued the novel because the critics feared that the popularity of novels as well as their growing mass public and female readership threatened the social order; by contrast, feminists, Derrideans, and other modern critics who revalue the novel oppose the marginal status to which the natural sciences have reduced the humanities since the 1960s.

These changing Anglo-American practices explain the revaluation of *Frankenstein*. Contrary accounts of *The Adventures of Huckleberry Finn*, which Chapter 4 discusses, suggest that these institutions have also developed a distinctly American orientation. Consider, for example, the novel's highly controversial depiction of racial differences. Some critics object not only that Huck, Pap, and others use the term "nigger" 213 times but also that in the minstrel fashion Twain depicts Jim and other blacks as darkies or as childlike, and, as a result, promotes white supremacy or, at the least, bad racial relations. Other critics grant that its characters have racist attitudes but claim that the novel satirizes or transcends them. Still others say that the novel resists Southern racism because Jim, who survives by his wits, was devoted to his family and a true father to Huck and because Huck decides to go to hell rather than turn Jim in or let him return to slavery.

What explains these and other, equally contrary, readings of the racial differences depicted by the novel? The answer lies not so much in the novel itself as in the ways in which modern American reading practices differ from those of the nineteenth century practices. Nineteenth-century reviewers and critics took the novel to represent a Dickensian realism allowing both the conservative affirmation and the liberal critique of the antebellum South. The Dickensian character of its realism was lost when, in keeping with the American studies programs emerging in the early twentieth century, Twain acquired the reputation of a genuine American personality and *Huckleberry Finn* the status of a great American novel. In the 1960s, the racial aspects of the novel became controversial not only because in the newly integrated American schools its readers included blacks and minorities but also because the emergence of academic criticism, including the black literary and cultural movements established in the 1960s and 1970s, justified critical reevaluations of the novel.

Since Twain acquired high status as a dramatic showman and public lecturer and reader, a number of critics dismiss such "academic" criticism as mere political correctness and emphasize his social or public import. Critics also emphasize the public status of Richard Wright's *Native Son* and dismiss its African American or multicultural versions, but they matter in this case too. As Chapter 6 indicates, the novel allows contrary readings, which include the well-established claim that *Native Son* is a naturalist protest novel inverting the ideals of detective fiction, as well as the equally well-established claim that *Native Son* depicts Bigger's existential struggle for liberation. Scholars attribute these incompatible views to Wright's changing beliefs; I will maintain, however, that, more than his beliefs, the changing status of naturalism and modernism and the emergence of black studies programs and of the modern university's cultural influence account for the contrary aspects of the novel. That is, in the twentieth century the modern university has acquired massive cultural influence that gives black scholars a new ability to mediate the public and private spheres and that explains not only why *Native Son's* naturalist version is incompatible with its modernist version but also why the black modernist version is progressive.

Contrary readings of Faulkner's *Light in August* and Morrison's *Jazz* also show the growing importance of black studies." Chapter 7 indicates, however, that in this case the contrary readings stem from black feminism's influence, including its postmodern dissolution of generic conventions and affirmation of the black community. In this vein it is interesting that, like *Frankenstein*, Faulkner's *Absalom, Absalom!* and Morrison's *Beloved* extend and rework the conventions of the gothic romance, which include multiple narrators, tormented lovers, dominating figures, spiritual exorcisms, and haunted houses, but, instead of heralding the triumph of good over evil or the victory of divine providence, these novels adopt the Aristotelian belief that the artistic imagination characterizes social life more profoundly than the mundane study of historical fact or providential design does. By contrast, more like Paretsky's mysteries than Shelley's *Frankenstein*, Faulkner's *Light in August* and Morrison's *Jazz* describe crimes and criminals in a realistic fashion, but instead of investigating at length who the culprit is or treating the culprit as demonic and the law as just, *Light in August* and *Jazz* problematize the identity of the culprits, who are outsiders or marginal figures unable to accept traditional middle-class or liberal values.

Although these novels both preserve an imaginative optimism whereby characters break with traditional racial and sexual categories and affirm themselves or improve their lives, the modernist *Light in August* expresses this optimism in an ambiguous fashion, whereas the postmodern *Jazz* adopts a decidedly optimistic view of them. The postmodern *Jazz* goes on, moreover, to dissolve the distinctions between the individual and the community, the narrator and the characters, and the city and the country. In an equally postmodern fashion, the mysteries of Sarah Paretsky dissolve the conventional distinction between popular culture, which conforms to its generic conventions and mainstream ideologies, and high art, which subverts them. As Chapter 7 suggests, Sarah Paretsky's mysteries, which have been very popular, with many weeks on the best-seller lists, publication in thirteen countries, and a worldwide network of fan clubs, do not show such conformity. What explains this popularity, according to feminists and others, is the fiction's critiques of its generic conventions and their enabling values or ideologies: the self-doubt, restrained sexuality, persistent investigation, community of friends, and social criticism of V.I. Warshawski, Paretsky's female detective-protagonist, subvert the liberal, middle-class faith whereby the detective-hero who preserves his or her certainty, impersonality, self-control, sexual intensity, and an anarchic or uncommitted lifestyle can restore justice to an unjust world. Moreover, because the sociohistorical conditions of American detective fiction readers, who used to be mainly male high school graduates but now include a growing number of college-educated women, have changed so markedly since the late nineteenth century, Paretsky's novels can challenge the conventions by which readers understand them and still achieve popularity.[6] The growth of college-educated women, who now attend in greater numbers than men do and who learn to value such challenges, enables the novels to break down the opposition between subversive high art, on the one hand, and established generic conventions, on the other, and, thereby, to mediate between the private academic and the public spheres.

A Brief History of Anglo-American Literary Criticism

As these accounts of *Frankenstein, Huckleberry Finn, Native Son, Light in August, Jazz,* and other works suggest, a Foucauldian approach reveals the historical conditions that have markedly expanded and transformed the ways in which Americans define and read literature in the last two hundred years. Scholars object, however, that such a Foucauldian method rejects the normative force of aesthetics or textual analysis and, as a result, accommodates the status quo.[7] I will discuss this objection more fully in the next chapter; for now, I can suggest that this method reveals the conflicted, local politics of reading practices.

What does the local politics of modern American reading practices consist of? They began in nineteenth-century Britain, when romantic writers defended the autonomy of the imagination or the genius of the great artist and rejected the historical methods of Samuel Johnson and other neoclassical critics, who accepted neoclassical ideals of decorum, propriety, and generic form on the grounds that they revealed the truths of social life. William Wordsworth maintained, for example, that the poet is "chiefly distinguished from other men by a greater promptness to think and feel . . . and a greater power to express such thoughts and feelings" ("Preface" 293). Similarly, Samuel T. Coleridge distinguished the imagination's finite repetition of the "infinite I am" from the fancy's generic or historical "fixities and definites" (313).

In addition, Wordsworth looked forward to the time when "the evil" of popular culture "will be systematically opposed, by men of greater powers" ("Preface" 288). Extending this appeal to "men of greater powers," Coleridge proposed a "clerisy" that would reformulate "sickly" middle-class reading practices. As Jon Klancher explains, the clerisy would resituate "the political state," reestablish "a state of intellectual grace," and restructure "the circulatory practices of reading and writing themselves" (164; 151–52).

Klancher adds that the clerisy "assumes the body of the humanist academy in the nineteenth and twentieth centuries"; however, in the late nineteenth century, when universities established departments of languages and literature, it was the scientific philologists who dominated, not the clerisy. The philologists resisted the romantics' defense of an autonomous imagination and preserved the neoclassical notion of generic types and biographical and historical contexts. They also adopted the broad cultural ideals whereby Greek and Roman literature represented what Matthew Arnold termed "the best that is thought and said in the world." Why did the philologists dominate? In the late eighteenth and early nineteenth centuries education turned popular because diverse institutions and organizations sought to regulate the health and the welfare of the population by, among other methods, educating them. As Ian Hunter explains, "The emergence in the early nineteenth century of a programme which linked national well-being to the intellectual and moral education of the 'popular classes' was . . . the result of the massing of a whole series of social surveys, reform campaigns, architectural innovations, evangelical movements, pedagogical theories and ethical imperatives" (183). Hunter says that this "'pedagogisation' of the social sphere" explains the domination of the philological method: "The old philologically based classical arts faculties were thus reorganised around a new core of ethical and intellectual disciplines, concentrated in the teaching of 'English' and history" (183–84).

Established in the 1890s, when American universities first became independent corporations and women, Jews, blacks, and others were disenfranchised, the philological method established the formal objectivity and neutrality of the humanities. For this reason and others, this method has remained central until the 1940s and 1950s, when literary study acquired the graduate programs, distinct fields, and professional associations and fostered formal methods and specialized research (Guillory, "Literary Study" 32–6). As literary study gained these new fields and associations in the post-WWII era, formal critics produced highly specialized readings and opposed the philologists' broad historical method, which, the formal critics said, did not explain a work's import or undertake close textual analyses of a text's figural devices (Graff 6–7).

This critique initiated the modern opposition of formal and historical methods. Some literary historians simply dismissed this critique, which they attributed to what Georg Lukács derisively labeled "shop talk" and E. D. Hirsch, Jr., called "cognitive atheism." Some historians sought more complex, textual accounts of a writer's style in order to reconcile the incompatible formal and historical approaches. Others also brought the formal and historical approaches together, but they established what Northrop Frye terms "objective" or purely "literary" methods and concepts and eventually opened literary study to poststructuralist or "New Historical" readings (see Graff 14–15 and 204–208). Still others promoted reader-response criticism in which, as Hans Robert Jauss says, the reader's constructive activity continually mediates literary study's "opposition between its aesthetic and its historical aspects" (19).

As the U.S. economy first achieved global dominance in the 1950s and 1960s and the university expanded rapidly, literary study allowed these and other versions of the antagonistic formal and historical opposition, which persists in modern literary study. In the 1980s and 1990s, when conservative politicians increasingly dominated federal and state government and the global economy was degrading American industry and finance, new conflicts, popularly termed "culture wars," were provoked by the explosive expansion of movies, television, the Internet, and other media; the university's populations of middle, working class, minority, and female students; and the humanities' disciplinary divisions and new black, women's, ethnic, gay, and postcolonial programs. These and other changes have virtually destroyed the ability of scholars and critics to set aside their academic character and address the general public in traditional ways. Conservatives and radicals alike objected, however, that, instead of influencing the public sphere, academic criticism irresponsibly ignores the needs of society or accommodates the corporate elites dominating the increasingly privatized university of the twenty-first century (see Rorty, *Achieving* 139; Brennan 12; Gitlin 152). Scholars as diverse as Allan Bloom, E. D. Hirsch, Jr., Gerald Graff, Fredric Jameson, Terry Eagleton, Sandra Gilbert and Susan Gubar, and Edward Said blamed the universities' expanding disciplines, their black, women's, or ethnic studies or their multicultural clientele for the humanities' growing fragmentation and declining public support. These scholars argued that, with its theoretical "jargon," subjective responses, and black, minority, and women's literatures, academic criticism alienates the public.

Defending the Arnoldian faith in the best that is "thought and said in the world," such arguments justify the objective philological method established in the 1890s, when women, blacks, and others were disenfranchised. In addition, as Patrick Brantlinger suggests, contemporary literary studies has grown marginal not because of women's or black literatures or theoretical jargon but because federal and state governments have reduced their financial support, students are increasingly majoring in technological and other job-related areas, the global economy is undermining the nation-state and the national cultures, and demand for writing programs has expanded, along with what Brantlinger terms "the pressure from new literatures in English" ("Who Killed" 22; see also Readings 465–83). Since the 1920s, the expanding commercial press, which has made fiction of all sorts very successful, has also increased the marginality of the humanities. The press has published short stories and serialized novels in mystery or romance magazines and in Sunday newspaper supplements, movie versions of popular novels helped make them bestsellers, and newsstands have made cheap paperbacks readily available (see Tebbel). In addition to the political and economic changes, this autonomy and ubiquity of popular culture have also rendered the traditional humanities marginal. Lastly, black, feminist, gay, ethnic, and postcolonial scholars work to overcome this marginality, not enforce it. As Richard Ohmanns shows, they "are in fact far more active and consequential now than in the early sixties . . . They work in different sites and in different ways" (75). These new ways of working give them the ability to influence their professional and nonprofessional communities and thereby to mediate between the university and the public.

Although the marginal status of the modern humanities stems from these political and economic changes and is mitigated by those scholars' new ways of working, this marginality has generated sharp, new debates about textual methods and historical, theoretical, or cultural approaches. In the previous debates, formal and historical critics were opposed, as were traditional and cultural or minority critics. Now, as I already noted, traditional critics also reject political, cultural, gay, feminist, or multicultural studies but justify textual and aesthetic criticism on the grounds that it preserves the normative force of literature and can, as a result, restore its lost influence. Sociohistorical or reader-oriented criticism, by contrast, rejects aesthetic norms and examines the reader's personality or historical context on the grounds that such study reaffirms literature's influence on the public sphere. As I argue in the next two chapters, the Foucauldian method overcomes this opposition of aesthetic and historical or reader-oriented methods. In the new social context, in which diverse cultural communities and programs mitigate the increasing marginality and isolation of the humanities, the historical study of modern reading practices explains and justifies the changing character of cultural study and at the same time effectively preserves the local autonomy of its aesthetic ideals.

CHAPTER 1

AESTHETIC THEORY

FROM MARXIST CRITIQUE TO CULTURAL HISTORY

ALTHOUGH THE CRITICAL THEORY OF THEODOR ADORNO HAS experienced a revival since the 1990s, what has been revived is not so much Adorno's Marxism as his aesthetics.[1] In keeping with the late twentieth-century movement defending aesthetic critique and rejecting sociohistorical and political analyses, critics take the critical negativity of his aesthetics to oppose the poststructuralist methods of Michel Foucault and others as well as the "identity politics" of feminists, gays, African Americans, and multiculturalists.[2] To an extent, the critics are right: in Adorno's view, instrumental reason imposes a repressive political domination on social institutions and grants subversive force to speculative theory or high art, not to the women's or the black liberation movement. Foucault, by contrast, rejects such aesthetic critique and describes the positive import and historical development or "genealogy" of governmental technologies, which supports, critics say, feminist or multicultural movements (see McNay and Sawicki). The trouble is, however, that Adorno's aesthetics and Foucault's genealogies parallel the onto-theology of Martin Heidegger and Jacques Derrida, what Adorno terms instrumental reason and Heidegger terms "equipmental" thinking in order to describe the customs, prejudices, or "being" dominating social life. These Heideggerian features of those theories generate an antinomy that opposes aesthetic critique and sociohistorical determination and that, as Chapter 2 suggests, pervades Heideggerian, neopragmatist, and post-Marxist cultural theory; however, the Foucauldian approach overcomes the antinomy, moving beyond Adorno's critical negativity, on the one hand, and sociohistorical determination, on the other.

THE AESTHETICS OF THEODOR ADORNO AND MARTIN HEIDEGGER

It is well known that Adorno and Horkheimer's influential account of the culture industry takes the contrary view. They argue that it turns readers, viewers, and audiences into supporters of the status quo. It promises to grant wishes, fulfill hopes, and realize desires, but it actually justifies the establishment. It is also well known that this view of the culture industry is justified by Adorno and Horkheimer's account of "instrumental reason," a notion which they derive from the Marxist Georg Lukács but explain in a Heideggerian manner. They argue that this rationality opposes mythological outlooks at the same time that it imposes an equally mythological faith in modern science and requires people to sacrifice themselves and repress their desires.

Less familiar are the parallels of Adorno's view of instrumental reason and Heidegger's view of technology. Heidegger says, for example, that, based on the mathematical calculation and systematic ordering of physical science, the essence of technology is to construe or "enframe" what exists exclusively as useful stock or "standing-reserve." Humanity "postures as the lord of the earth" but, failing to grasp "this enframing as a claim," stands "in subservience to it" ("Technology" 332). In other words, "the essence of modern technology" is to deny humans their sense of self or identity. As I noted, Adorno and Horkheimer also argue that, produced by the Enlightenment, instrumental reason makes humanity subservient because it imposes a mythological faith in modern science at the same time that it opposes mythological outlooks. Contrary to mythology, science maintains that humanity, not the gods, rules nature, yet "myths already entail enlightenment" because both mythology and science presuppose that knowledge enables knowers to dominate nature and people by repressing their desires or sacrificing themselves. In the name of facts and laws, the enlightenment dismisses the magic and fantasy of myth, but enlightenment still "entangles itself in mythology" by exacting sacrifices from the enlightened and endowing established social structures with a mythical inevitability (27).

Jameson denies that Adorno's view of instrumental reason parallels Heidegger's view of technology on the grounds that "Error, what is called metaphysics or identity, is in Adorno the effect of an increasingly powerful social system, while in Heidegger it is that of an increasing distance from some original truth" (10).[3] It is true that in Heidegger's but not in Adorno's view Western society had the capacity to experience the poetic "shining of truth" but lost it in the classical Greek era. It is also true that Adorno forcefully condemns Heidegger's notion of Being because he dismisses its "jargon of authenticity" as well as Heidegger's fascist politics. Heidegger claims, nonetheless, that since the Greek era the Western tradition's propositional and equipmental or technological modes of understanding dominate, producing the presence of beings but not of what, like Aristotle, he calls Being or what is. Similarly, Adorno and Horkheimer say that instrumental rationality not only dominates capitalism and communism, it also began with the Greeks. They show, for example, that, when Homer's Ulysses resists the sirens, his resistance underlines the Greek mastery of nature; "Measures like those taken on Odysseus's ship in face of the Sirens are a prescient allegory of the dialectic of Enlightenment" (27). The mastery of nature, along with opposition to mythology, characterizes the propositional logic and conceptual discourse of both the Greeks and the modern enlightenment. As Bernstein says, "In Heidegger's fateful, strong reading of the 'history of being' . . . we find a thematic affinity with Adorno's claim that the seeds of 'identity logic' with its hidden will-to-mastery are to be found in the very origins of Western rationality" (*Fate* 198).[4]

What is more, Adorno's view of art also parallels Heidegger's view. In the *Dialectic of Enlightenment* Adorno and Horkheimer say, for example, that, divided and contradictory, high art accepts and subverts established aesthetic practices and ruling ideologies, resists its commodified character, and, as a negative moment projecting a utopian vision, reaffirms the totality (see *Dialectic* 120–67; Eagleton, *Ideology* 356–57). In *Language, Poetry, Thought* and other later work, Heidegger also attributes to art a divided or conflicted character: great art reveals and conceals Being, disclosing and hiding truth. In this conflicted text, what Heidegger terms "Earth," which denotes both the work's concrete materials as well as a perspective that puts them into place, resists "World," which is not only the meaning of the work but also the coherence and totality achieved by it. As the "open," Being comes into the "clearing" established in the work, yet Being also remains hidden, for Earth "juts" into World, setting World into itself. Since the work cannot disclose Being without concealing it, neither Earth nor World achieve mastery. As Richard Bernstein points out, Adorno's claim that texts betray unresolved conflicts and oppositions implicitly describing society's hidden totality parallels this strife of Earth and World: "The strife . . . becomes a general characterization for the relation of elements in a totality which can then be projected onto a community" (*Fate* 124).

Adorno's view of instrumental reason and of high art parallels Heidegger's view, yet Adorno's view derives from the Marxist Georg Lukács, not from Heidegger.[5] Revising and extending Karl Marx's critique of commodity fetishism, Lukács argues that capitalism extends the commodity's domination, ensuring that instrumental reason, which calculates means and not ends, evaluates techniques and not values, and seeks autonomy and not community, governs bourgeois social and economic institutions. Once economic institutions gain their independence, capitalism imposes this rationality on all realms, including the intellectual (see Bernstein, *Philosophy* 82).

In the influential essay "Reification and the Consciousness of the Proletariat," Lukács goes on, however, to defend the revolutionary potential of the working class. In 1921, when the Soviet revolution was flowering and Western revolutions looked possible, an optimistic Lukács maintained that the working class is "the identical subject-object of the social and historical processes of evolution" (149). In the 1950s, when the Stalinist tyranny was ending, he argued that history would eventually culminate in full communism, which unites and reconciles the fragmented subject with itself. On this basis he defends the realist novel, whose typical characters and broad class contexts show that the subject passes through distinct, historical stages, its alienation and fragmentation coming to an end only in the communist era.

Adorno and Horkheimer also assume that instrumental reason dominates bourgeois social life and that Hegelian theory undermines it; with fascism recently defeated, the cold war underway, and the capitalist economy booming, they maintain, however, that instrumental rationality assimilates all opposition, including the working class and the communists, who also impose the oppressive domination of Enlightenment rationality. In addition, in the Heideggerian fashion they claim that instrumental rationality does not begin with the capitalist system, as Lukács says; it begins with the classical Greeks. Lastly, Adorno denies that at history's end the fragmented subject will be reconciled with itself. He claims that, on the contrary, the Hegelian dialectical reconciliation of subject and object itself represents the domination of Enlightenment reason. Purely conceptual, this reconciliation imposes an abstract identity that denies the subject's concrete particularity. While Lukács adapts an absolutist view in which realist art shows that historical development culminates in communism, which reconciles subject and object, Adorno maintains that the non-identity of subject and object liberates art, preserving its autonomy by dividing form and content and allowing many different totalities. As he says of Hegel, "Nowhere does he define the experience of the non-identical as the *telos* of the aesthetic subject or as its emancipation" (Adorno 113).

Although Adorno derives his view of instrumental reason from Lukács, Adorno rejects Lukács's faith in the working class, communism, and historical progress. Jameson argues, however, that these rejections do not matter, because he divides political action, class struggle, and sequential social formations into three distinct "frameworks" (*The Political Unconscious* 78–79). Since Adorno's Marxism has to do, he says, with the third framework, social formations, not with the first, political activity, or the second, class struggle, these frameworks justify Adorno's view: "This recognition [e.g., of the frameworks] was meant, if not to solve, at least to neutralize, what seemed to me false problems and meaningless polemics . . . where proponents of an active, shaping role of working people seemed to confront those for whom disembodied forces and logic of capital were somehow at work" (*Late* 8).

On these ontological grounds not only does Jameson "neutralize" these "false problems and meaningless polemics," he reconciles the incompatible methods of Adorno and

Lukács, putting together Adorno's aesthetic critique of social life and Lukács's historical evolution of periods. He assumes, in other words, that an artist's or a text's subversion of social life, ideological practices, or artistic or cultural conventions goes together with a text's representing high realism, modernism, postmodernism, or other periods, which are objectively mapped by the artist's unconscious mind. Peter Osborne says, however, that this reconciliation is contradictory: "The best of both worlds (a philosophically self-enclosed hermeneutics and a sociologically and politically open form of historical criticism) is simply not available without contradiction"(191). Osborne is right; however, what justifies this reconciliation of contrary methods is the ontological claim that aesthetic critique occupies one level and historical development another level, not the logic of the methods. In the Hegelian's big picture or totality, these levels go together because differences are cancelled and preserved. Yet it is just that Hegelian ontology that Adorno rejects in the name of singularity and non-identity.

Although Adorno's view of instrumental reason has Marxist roots, his view parallels Heidegger's notion of technology because Adorno rejects Marxism's Hegelian faith in communism, class struggle, and historical progress. Derrida rejects Heidegger's notion of Being as well as Adorno's Marxism, but he too critiques Western metaphysics in a Heideggerian fashion. For example, Derrida argues, as Adorno does, that Marxism does not escape Western reason or onto-theology. Adorno claims that in the Enlightenment fashion Marxism claims to master nature and humanity but fails to exclude mythology or to enable liberation; similarly, Derrida says that Marxism means to depict history scientifically but does not exclude its spectral others. Marx critiques not only the spirit or specter but also ideology and commodity fetishism, but his critique fails to exclude these spectral others because they are already within Marxism, part of Marx's revolutionary spirit or communist movement. Both Derrida and Adorno maintain, moreover, that communism is a utopian vision, not a practical enterprise. Adorno says that art reaffirms the totality as a negative moment projecting a utopian vision. Derrida adopts a "messianic" concept of justice, rather than this subversive aesthetic totality; he claims, nonetheless, that in a utopian fashion this messianism affirms an absolute hospitality to a religious or messianic other, including the dead.

This critique of Marxism suggests that Derrida's account of Western metaphysics preserves the negativity that Adorno and Heidegger share. Derrida's account is, just the same, largely textual. For instance, Heidegger and Derrida both critique the onto-theological tradition, which assumes that language serves the ends of thought. Heidegger argues, however, that, as a "happening," revelation, or "unconcealment," not a propositional or factual assertion, art brings "what is" "into the Open" (36). In the influential essay "Différance," Derrida, speaking of all writing, not just art, also says that it purports to reveal Being or Truth, but, instead of doing so, writing generates it as a discursive effect or differs it indefinitely. As the inaudible "a" in "différance" suggests, writing generates textual effects that Heidegger (mis)construes as the venerable presence of "Being."

On these textual grounds Derrida critiques not only Heidegger's notion of Being but also the realism that Heidegger and Adorno share. In *Truth in Painting*, he points out, for example, that, to critique what Heidegger terms the "workly" character of the work, the "thingly" character of the thing, or the "equipmental" character of equipment, he draws on Kant's notion of enframing, which says that philosophy establishes what is intrinsic and extrinsic to a work or where its border or framework lies. Although this notion of enframing opens a text's various constructions to aesthetic critique and, as I will argue, to a Foucauldian appropriation,

Heidegger inconsistently preserves a text's realism. He claims, for example, that the pair of shoes depicted by one of Van Gogh's paintings are peasant shoes. Derrida, who doubts that the shoes are a pair, objects to this claim as well as the contrary claim of Meyer Shapiro, the art historian who says that the shoes belong to Van Gogh, not to a peasant. Such claims naively assume, Derrida says, that the shoes possess a "precritical or pretextual reality." The frame of the painting, which gives it an inside and an outside, should reveal what the shoes are "in truth," but the pretextual reality that Heidegger attributes to them gives them an independent "character" or "subject" (286–87).

Faulting Hegelian or Marxist realism in a similar way, Derrida adds that, "on the pretext of delivering you from the chains of writing and reading," those who "hastily lock you up in a supposed outside of the text: the pre-text of perception, of living speech . . . of real history . . . try to intimidate you, to subject you to the oldest, most dogmatic, most sinisterly authoritarian program, to the most massive mediating machines" (326). This objection to "real history" and "massive mediating machines" forcefully debunks not only Heidegger's notion of Being but also Adorno's Marxist realism. As Bernstein says, putting the point in traditional terms, Derrida rejects Adorno's belief that art imitates an incomprehensible reality (*Fate* 218).

Eagleton grants that Adorno and Derrida fully appreciate nonidentity, multiplicity, and difference but maintains that, unlike Derrida and other poststructuralists, Adorno recognizes as well the positive identity and human values in art because he remains realist.[6] It is true that Foucault and Derrida both fault the realism or ontological truth of Heidegger's notion of Being and Adorno's speculative dialectics, yet their critiques have positive import. Thanks to them, Derrida establishes a textual aesthetics and, as I will now show, Foucault develops an historical ontology.

Certainly Foucault, who late in his life called Heidegger "an overwhelming influence" on his work (cited in Schwartz 163), also develops a Heideggerian account of technological practices that rejects the realism that Heidegger and Adorno share.[7] He claims, however, that changing paradigms or epistemes explain the history or the influence of discourse. His archaeologies of madness, punishment, and sexuality examine the positive historical paradigms explaining how the treatments of the mad, prisoners, or sexual perversity have changed. His later work, which is genealogical, not archaeological, examines the ruptured evolution of the technology by which various institutions or discourses constitute or regulate the subject. As strategies with dispositions and techniques, these discourses form a complex that Foucault terms governmentality and that organize or regulate diverse institutions in equally diverse or discontinuous ways. Adorno and Heidegger also produce genealogies of technological or instrumental reason explaining its Greek origins and its domination of modern society, but they claim that, because of it, Being has been forgotten, and modern cultural life produces only ideological conformity and intellectual vacuity. Foucault shows, by contrast, that a genealogy recounts the internal divisions or conflicts of a particular discourse and depicts, as a result, its discontinuous, fragmented, but positive history, rather than a repressive and monolithic tradition.[8]

Although Foucault develops the Heideggerian notion that the equipmental or technological reason constitutes the subject, he interprets these technologies in historical terms according to which diverse genealogies of the subject undermine instrumental reason or the onto-theological tradition. In *The Hermeneutics of the Subject* and other essays, Foucault argues, for example, that the onto-theological tradition of Heidegger and Derrida (and the parallel instrumental reason of Adorno) take the ethics of Plato to ground the Western metaphysical tradition, but the diverse genealogies of the Greek, Stoic, Christian, and Cartesian ethics subvert this monolithic account and impose divergent practices and activities.

Foucault shows, for example, that the Greeks, the Romans, the Christians, and the moderns develop an ethics of care whose contrary features are incompatible with a monolithic theological tradition or instrumental reason. The Socratic ethics of the Greeks requires a knowledge of the self enabling the individual to control his or her desires, achieve maturity, and join the polis. The Socratic ethics involves, in addition, a personal, intimate, dialectics that excludes writing, rhetoric, and the many, and, as the Heideggerians show, privileges speech, concepts, and the one, universal truth. The Romans' stoic ethics also requires a knowledge of the self enabling the individual to control his or her desires, but the stoic ethics extends to the individual's whole life and preserves his or her independence. Moreover, this ethics grants writing a place in its sexual discourse and in that way breaks with Plato'saccount of speech, presence, and truth ("Hermeneutics" 100–101; see also Paul Allen Miller 61). The Christian pastoral also elaborates an ethics of self-fashioning, but this ethics, which treats the desires of the self as sinful or guilty, renounces the self. The individual examines himself to determine if his thoughts or wishes show the corrupting influence of Satan, not the regulation of his desires or the preservation of his autonomy ("On the Genealogy of Ethics" 361). Lastly, contrary to Derrida, who treats *The Meditations* of Descartes as a formal argument, *The Meditations* establish a modern ethics in which care of the self gives way to knowledge of the self, whereby anyone who can grasp the facts can gain knowledge of his or her true self ("Genealogy" 371–72).[9]

Foucault maintains that such diverse genealogies of the subject undermine instrumental reason or the onto-theological tradition and impose divergent practices, whereas, despite many differences, Adorno, Heidegger, and Derrida claim that equipmental or instrumental reason or the onto-theological tradition exerts an oppressive influence that only the subversive negativity of writing/art overcomes. In other words, the Heideggerian work of Adorno, Derrida, and Foucault generates an antinomy in which aesthetic negativity and instrumental reason or the onto-theological tradition oppose the divergent technologies of social or institutional histories. In the next chapter, I will argue, however, that a Foucauldian aesthetics can escape the opposition. As John Frow suggests, such an aesthetics preserves the textual grounds of reading or interpretation, but cultural technologies, what Frow terms "regimes of reading," still construct the relationship of text and reader. First I will show, however, that this antinomy pervades Heideggerian cultural theory, which includes the reception aesthetics of Wolfgang Iser and Hans Robert Jauss, the neopragmatism of Stanley Fish and Steven Mailloux, and the post-Marxism of Tony Bennett, John Frow, Pierre Macherey, and Jacques Rancière.

CHAPTER 2

AESTHETICS AND READING

BETWEEN THEORY AND HISTORY

As I indicated in the last chapter, Foucault develops the Heideggerian notion that equipmental or technological reason constitutes the subject, but he interprets this technology in historical terms, according to which diverse genealogies of the subject undermine instrumental reason or the onto-theological tradition. Despite many differences, Adorno, Heidegger, and Derrida claim, by contrast, that the subversive negativity of writing or art, not governmental technologies, overcomes the oppressive influence of equipmental or instrumental reason. In other words, the Heideggerian work of Adorno, Derrida, and Foucault generates an antinomy in which aesthetic critique opposes positive social or historical genealogies of the subject. In this chapter, I will argue that a Foucauldian aesthetics can escape the antinomy, preserving the aesthetic negativity of Heideggerian aesthetics, especially its ability to affirm and undermine a text's interpretations, as well as the sociohistorical regimes, communities, or reading formations governing the practices of readers. First I will show, however, that this antinomy pervades Heideggerian cultural theory, which includes the reception aesthetics of

Wolfgang Iser and Hans Robert Jauss, the neopragmatism of Stanley Fish and Steven Mailloux, the Foucauldian historicism of Pierre Macherey and Jacques Rancière, and the post-Marxism of Tony Bennett and John Frow.

WOLFGANG ISER AND HANS ROBERT JAUSS: FROM READING TO AESTHETICS

Iser and Jauss emphasize the importance of the reader's interpretive practices but defend the Heideggerian notion that that aesthetic theory liberates the human self from oppressive social institutions. In early work, Iser and Jauss both maintain, for example, that great art moves the reader to set aside his or her preconceptions and produce a disturbing interpretation. Iser adopts the Heidegger's notion that a text—an event or "happening"—both reveals and conceals being, disclosing and hiding truth. In *The Act of Reading* (1977), Iser maintains, for example, that, moved by the text to synthesize what he calls "perspectives" derived from the text's narrator, characters, plot, themes, and fictitious reader, readers arrive at an interpretation that changes them. The normative text signals, guides, directs, and manipulates readers. Iser claims, nonetheless, that readers produce their own textual structure or object.

The potentials, perspectives, segments, or sequences of the text are connected by indeterminate gaps, blanks, discrepancies, and absences that disturb the structure and stimulate the reader's activity (*Act* 98–99). These gaps, blanks, and disturbances of the many-layered, literary text undermine the reader's conventions, moving the reader to reinterpret the text and, more importantly, to produce what it cannot—the experience of a coherent whole growing out of "the alteration or falsification of that which is already ours" (*Act* 132).

Jauss also says that the text moves the reader to break with his or her preconceptions, but he adopts the hermeneutics of Hans Georg Gadamer, Heidegger's student. That is, he claims that hermeneutic understanding requires a dialog of self and other, rather than a transformative interpretation of the text's blanks and gaps. In the influential essay, "Literary History as a Challenge to Literary Theory," Jauss insists that the meaning of a text, especially an ancient one, is not immediately or empirically given to an objective scholar, who has only to set aside his biases to grasp what the text shows; rather, because time and change sharply divide the perspective or horizon of the reader from that of the author, interpretation involves a dialog in which the text poses a question to which the reader provides an answer. Since this dialog moves the reader to break with his conventions and grasp those of the author's perspective, the dialog enables the reader to mediate between his own time or perspective and that of the alien text or author.

This approach explains the dialectical relationship of the historical author's and the modern reader's horizons. Moreover, in later work Jauss limits the transformative power of aesthetic norms. He argues that, contrary to Adorno, aesthetic negativity does not deny the reader's pleasure and cathartic emotions or enable commodity production to coopt the reader, rendering him or her useful and cooperative (*Aesthetic Experience* 18–19). In later work, Iser, by contrast, extends the subversive negativity of aesthetics. Dividing literature into the fictive (what gives literature its shape) and the imaginary (what provides its amorphous stuff), Iser argues that the fictive and the imaginary both exclude and preserve reality. As Anglo-American philosophy has demonstrated, literature plays a positive role in understanding and even constituting reality and simultaneously a negative role in subverting it.

Fiction and the imaginary play various productive roles in philosophy and everyday life at the same time that they resist such limiting roles and remain indefinable. What enables fiction and the imaginary to escape these roles is the dialectical play whereby fiction and the imaginary determine each other. In Iser's terms, "By opening up spaces of play, the fictive compels the imaginary to take on a form at the same time that it acts as a medium for its manifestation" (*Fictive* xvii).

In later work, Jauss also says that the fictive and the imaginary determine each other and that they both exclude and constitute reality, as Iser claims. He argues, nonetheless, that the imaginary evolves from the classical era, when it provided religious or mystic experience of the perfect, to the modern era, which resists such closed notions of the perfect. On these historical grounds, he claims that the aesthetic negativity of literature is limited to modernist art (*Aesthetic Experience* 18–19).

Iser not only insists, by contrast, that the negativity and subversive doubling of literature constitute and resist the real, but also argues that literature produces a new human plasticity or new possibilities.[1] Although this literary subversion does not undermine the technological, equipmental, or instrumental rationality that, according to Heidegger and Adorno, dominate modern life, the subversion dismisses literature's institutional status, which, as I noted, include literature's established canons of great works, its schools of interpretation, and its place in a country's cultural offices. As Iser says, "literature becomes a panorama of what is possible, because it is not hedged in either by the limitations or the considerations that determine the institutionalized organizations within which human life otherwise takes its course" (*Fictive* 297).

THE NEOPRAGMATISM OF STANLEY
FISH AND STEVEN MAILLOUX

The reception study of Fish and Mailloux also examines the interpretive activity of readers or critics but, instead of defending the transformative force of aesthetic ideals, as Iser does, Fish and Mailloux reject the foundational status of aesthetics and in a Foucauldian manner take the reader's cultural contexts to regulate his or her interpretive practices.

Like Jauss, Mailloux adopts the Heideggerian hermeneutics of Gadamer, who claims that "understanding" interprets the text from the interpreter's perspective, tradition, or horizon. Mailloux assumes, however, that the reader's traditions include the rhetoric defended by the Greek sophists and by modern pragmatists. More importantly, he claims that, far from preserving the historical continuity of aesthetic traditions, different readers produce different interpretations and even different texts because diverse rhetorical conventions govern their interpretive practices.

Similarly, in the early "The Affective Fallacy Fallacy," Fish, like Iser, adopts a Heideggerian perspective in which reading is a temporal process in which the reader constructs interpretations and, when they mislead him or her, repudiates them in favor of new ones.[2] In later work, Fish too maintains that diverse rhetorical conventions govern the reader's practices, but he adopts the Foucauldian assumption that what determines the validity of the reader's interpretation is the reader's "interpretive community." This community he defines as a group of scholars who, like New Critics, authorial humanists, phenomenologists, structuralists, Derrideans, feminists, and Marxists, accept and apply a common set of conventions (*Is There* 171).

In the Heideggerian fashion, Iser says that a text's norms or literature's doubling or other aesthetic devices limit interpretive practices and change the reader's outlook, whereas both Fish and Mailloux adopt the Foucauldian belief that the interpretive or rhetorical practices of a community or discipline justify or limit the reader's interpretive practice. Moreover, both Mailloux and Fish deny the transformative force of aesthetic norms. Fish admits that theorists may examine the rhetorical figures of a text, the unifying intention of its author, its play of gender differences, or its critiques of ideology; however, in the pragmatist fashion he treats these diverse interpretive practices as a matter of local, Derridean, authorial, feminist, or Marxist beliefs, not of valid theory, which, he says, does not ensure a reader's self-consciousness, govern interpretive practice, or change anything at all ("Consequences" 437).

Mailloux also considers aesthetic theory nonfoundational, but he favors the sophistic rhetoric of Protagorus, who in Plato's famous dialog claims that man is the measure of all things. Taken as social and not as individual, Protagorus's claim implies, Mailloux says, that "all we have to deal with as situated observers are the webs of belief and desire that constitute our rhetorical contexts" ("Articulation" 12). Hence, he concludes that no privileged standpoint enables us to consider our aesthetic or ultural norms superior to others or to stigmatize our cultural others.

Iser too considers his aesthetic theory nonfoundational, but by "foundational" he means pragmatic, empirical, or conceptual discourses that give imagination or fiction a definition, purpose, or context. Speaking of imagination as fantasy, he says, for example, "A glance at foundational discourses reveals an unmistakable reduction, whereby fantasy is always subordinated to something else" (*Fictive* 171). This claim implies that a nonfoundational view of the imagination resists such conceptualization and achieves an autonomy that, in Iser's anthropological terms, expresses a nonessentialist human plasticity.

In short, Iser's reception aesthetics emphasizes literature's autonomy and subversive negativity, while the reception study of Fish and Mailloux limits the transformative powers of aesthetic theory and acknowledges the professional or rhetorical contexts of modern literary study. As Winfried Fluck suggests, these contrary approaches implicitly reformulate the Heideggerian antinomy of aesthetic negativity and social determination: in her negative formulation, those who doubt "the unquestioned authority of the concept of the aesthetic" mean "to erase the difference between politics and aesthetics, so that literary texts can have a direct political function and the profession of literary criticism can be redefined as political work" ("Aesthetics" 93).

Historical Accounts of Aesthetics

Like Fish and Mailloux, Macherey and Rancière also explain aesthetics in a Foucauldian fashion, but, preserving this antinomy, they describe the conflicts and oppositions driving the historical evolution of aesthetic practices, not the aesthetic norms governing or transforming the reader. Initially Macherey defended an Althusserian Marxist criticism, in which the ordinary reader falls victim to ideology, whose hidden purposes he inadvertently carries out, whereas the critic who adopts a scientific Marxism discovers the ideological import of the gaps created by literary production and in that way gains objective knowledge of history (*Towards* 1–14). Subsequently, Macherey, Foucault's fellow student and colleague at France's elite École Normale Supérieure, rejects this Marxism, explains the emergence and evolution of new epistemes, and frees the critic to resist the text's historical contexts. Rancière also rejects his earlier support of Althusserian Marxism and explains this evolution but he examines the "democratic" writing practice undermining the regimes' hierarchic organization and giving excluded groups a voice.

Since Macherey was, he says, "particularly stimulated" by Foucault's notion of an episteme (see *dinosaure* 167–68), he examines the archive of conventions and norms elaborated by artistic works. He claims, for example, that Hugo's *Les Misérables* describes society as a sea in which, like the night, uncertain characters appear and disappear (*Object* 90–92). He says that this description takes for granted an episteme in which a subterranean man emerges from a tumultuous society. Created by the press and elaborated from 1840 to 1850, this episteme informs the work of the radical Karl Marx, the conservative Alexis de Tocqueville, as well as liberal social theorists.

Similarly, Madame de Staël imposed on the French the "creative" belief that Immanuel Kant reconciles sentiment and reflection and, thereby, defends an obscure, formal, but still vital kind of "philosophical enthusiasm" (*Object* 28–29). She created what he considers an original and influential view of German culture, according to which the "enthusiastic" philosophical spirit of the Germans forcefully reconciles the heart and the mind, or the universal concept and the concrete reality, but the fragmented character of the German nation isolates the Germans, rendering them abstract, sectarian, and impractical (*Object* 30–35).

Although Macherey describes the emergence and influence of such epistemes, he defends, just the same, a revised version of Marxist materialism. He grants that the "materialist" core of Hegel's idealist dialectics is, as Marx and Engels claimed, "'wrapped' in a teleological discourse of a unitary nature affirming the ineluctable reconciliation of . . . opposites"

(*Materialist* 141). He maintains, however, that they got his idealism wrong: as he says, "Their blunder corresponds precisely to the illusion of an independent theoretical knowledge, realized in the form of a doctrinaire materialism" (*Materialist* 141). Since the history of philosophy includes diverse and contrary systems in contradiction with each other, as Hegel claimed, a materialist theory explains their systematic oppositions as well the evolving archives of cultural conventions

Rancière also maintains that an aesthetic regime of conventions and norms, what he terms a distribution (*partage*) of the sensible, governs the history of art or philosophy. He argues, however, that politics as a democratizing process whereby the excluded classes and groups struggle for comprehension and equality, while regulatory forces, aptly labeled the "police," resist this struggle and preserve society's hierarchic order. Analogous to society's political conflicts, the internal opposition of the regime and writing, not the systematic contradictions of Hegelian Marxism, explain this evolution. In his account, a regime of conventions and norms, what he terms a distribution (partage), construct and reconstruct the political communities that organize the work or labor of society. At the same time, the regimes fail to limit writing, whose wandering, rootless "democratic" character undermines them.

For example, in what he calls a classical or poetic regime, "high genres" were, he says, "devoted to the imitation of noble actions and characters, and low genres were devoted to common people and base subject matters. The hierarchy of genres also submitted style to a principle of propriety(*convenance*): kings had to act and speak as kings do, and common people as common people do" ("Politics" 13). By contrast, what he terms the representative regime rejects the poetic regime's hierarchical schema of classification. Indifferent to the objects it depicts, this regime describes representative or mimetic ways of organizing ways of doing, seeing, and judging any objects, not just proper or appropriate ones. Lastly, the aesthetic regime identifies art not by its means of creating or representing objects but by a mode of sensibility proper to artistic products but estranged from itself (*Partage* 30–31).

Macherey also explains the evolution of cultural practices, but he argues, as Iser and Jauss do, that readers may break with the author's context and pursue their own concerns. On the one hand, he claims that literary criticism that takes the historical context of the author as the work's ontological or realist truth reduces the work to "dead fruit." Adopted by Marx, Hegel, and Sartre, this criticism says that the reader can bring an old work to life only if he or she enters into or recreates the divided historical context of the dead author. On the other hand, he argues that Foucault frees the work from this existence as a relic. Not only does Foucault critique the notion that the work is a mirror in which author and reader construct a relationship giving the author a "feigned objectivity," he also suggests that texts acquire reality or existence when readers reproduce them, not when writers produce them. As Macherey says, "If one takes this hypothesis seriously, one must go so far as to say that works are not at all 'produced' as such, but begin to exist only from the moment they are 'reproduced'" (*Materialist* 47).

Rancière, by contrast, considers the aesthetic regimes normative or regulatory; as Bennett points out, they enable governments to promote the liberal technology of self-rule. What explains their evolution is the oppositions that result from writing's democratic character and that the regimes have, since the *Republic* of Plato, tried to resolve only to generate new contradictions or to reproduce the old contradictions in new ways.

In *La Parole Muette*, he suggests, for example, that these contradictions explain the "slow revolution" whereby literature evolves from "a state of knowledge that lets one speak as a connoisseur of works of Belles-Lettres" to a state in which, "under the sign of a rock, a desert, and the sacred," literature provides "a radical experience of language devoted to the production of silence" (9; my translation). In this evolution, the representative regime overturns the classical regime, in which literature represents or imitates reality and the critic speaks as a knowledgeable connoisseur, and construes literature as the romantic expression of the artistic will. As a result, the representative regime faces problems with writing whose anarchic, rootless or wandering character the classical hierarchies opposed. The representative regime also faces contradictions of its own, since its indifference to the objects of its expression is not, Rancière says, consistent with its belief that the substance of art is language. The aesthetic regime, which extends and opposes the representative regime, dismisses literature's material body and construes it as vision or music but ultimately treats the literature as a material entity in its own right.

While Macherey describes the systematic contradictions explaining the evolution of cultural discourse, his materialism frees the reader to resist the text's historical contexts and to explore his or her own preconceptions. The aesthetic regimes of Rancière regulate readers, writers, and social practices, but he emphasizes the internal conflicts and tensions whereby "democratic" writing practices undermine the hierarchic organization imposed by aesthetic regimes and develop internal contradictions explaining their evolution.

THE POST-MARXISM OF
TONY BENNETT AND JOHN FROW

Like Macherey and Rancière, Bennett and Frow adopt a Foucauldian approach explaining the historical evolution of cultural institutions. Like Stanley Fish and Steven Mailloux, who say that the interpretive community or rhetorical conventions of the reader explain his or her interpretive activity, Bennett and Frow claim that "reading formations" or "regimes of reading" govern the reader, but these formations or regimes are not speculative constructs implicit in the text's language or the reader's rhetoric; they are established in educational or cultural institutions, and, in Frow's textual version, they overcome the Heideggerian antinomy of aesthetics and social determination.

Initially Bennett and Frow favor Althusserian Marxism, in which the ordinary reader falls victim to the text's ideology because it presents itself as historical truth, whereas the rigorous, scientific critic recognizes the formal gaps and aesthetic incoherence whereby the work reveals its ideological import (see Macherey, *A Theory* 1–14). This notion of scientific criticism echoes the views of Heidegger, Iser, and Jauss, who also say that in the text the "space of gap and play" enables readers to mediate between their historical contexts and the text's or the author's contexts. Also like Iser and Jauss, Bennett and Frow suggest that reading constitutes the text's references to codes, genres, other texts, and nonliterary discourses, but they adopt Russian formalist concepts of defamiliarization, estrangement, or intertextuality because Russian formalism subverts traditional notions of autonomous historical truth and, as a result, opens texts to the activities of readers and their changing cultural contexts.[3]

In later work Bennett argues that the reading formations that maintain the aesthetic norms of the text and the ideal of the reader's self-improvement are embedded in authoritative cultural institutions. Rancière shows that, because of writing's democratic character, aesthetic regimes develop internal contradictions explaining their evolution, but Bennett considers them positive cultural technologies that promote the liberal technology of self-rule and thereby improve social life.

He argues, moreover, that various technologies produce various cultural resources and impose equally various forms and kinds of discipline or governmental organization (69–70). Not only schools but also libraries and museums impose such norms.

Moreover, like Fish and Mailloux, he debunks "foundational" aesthetics, but he argues that the traditional aesthetics of David Hume, Immanuel Kant, and other modern theorists requires but fails to establish absolute norms of universal value. He repudiates the aesthetics of the Frankfurt School because it reduces cultural institutions to a political instrument or to a threatening co-optation. He also repudiates the Marxist aesthetics of Raymond Williams, who denied that aesthetic ideals transcend their historical context and construed culture as a whole way of life. Bennett complains that, despite this denial he preserved the romantic quest for an ideal aesthetic wholeness, which he expected history to restore (*Science* 21–5).

Like Bennett, Fish, and Mailloux, Frow takes "regimes of reading" to govern the interpretive activities of readers; however, like Macherey, he does not accept their regulatory or normative character. He claims, for example, that different types of art—high art, popular or mass art, men's or women's art, various subcultures' art—assume different criteria or "regimes" of value. To apply a universal criteria to them or to consider different kinds of art commensurable is to devalue those practices that "fail to measure up" (*Studies* 132). Frow adds that to insist upon a "single scale" or a "uniform criterion" is not to transform the reader but to repress "the differences and specificity of other practices" (*Studies* 132).

Moreover, unlike Bennett, Fish, and Mailloux, who reject the normative or foundational character of aesthetics, he preserves aesthetic self-consciousness because he fears that these incommensurable regimes generate a vitiating relativism that renders all judgments of value equivalent, ignores differences within communities, and permits no "*critique* of everyday processes" (*Studies* 132). Such aesthetic self-consciousness would, he claims, enable "cultural intellectuals" to grasp their determining sociohistorical interests as a class (*Studies* 165–69), and readers to resist the established codes, genres, and norms of their regimes of reading; as he says, "The productive role of the reader . . . represents a break with a dominant regime of reading and with the institutional context which directly or indirectly sustains this regime" (*Marxism* 229).

The claim that the aesthetic self-consciousness of intellectuals and readers enables them to "break with . . . the institutional context" of literary study contradicts the Foucauldian belief that, as a "regime of reading," that context governs their interpretive practice. Frow would seem to have it both ways. He goes on, however, to deny that these regimes have what he terms a direct "expressive relation" to social groups: "Cultural regimes are relatively autonomous of social groups, and do not represent them in the sense of bearing or expressing their essential interests" ("*On*" 52). If cultural regimes do not reduce to or represent cultural technologies, they do not preclude aesthetic self-consciousness.

They do not exclude, in particular, Derrida's critique of Kant's aesthetic frame or parergon, which, as I noted in Chapter 1, says that philosophy establishes what is intrinsic and extrinsic to a work or where its border or framework lies. Revising this critique of Kant, Frow argues that "textuality and its conditions of possibility are mutually constitutive and can be reconstructed only from each other in a kind of hermeneutic bootstrapping" ("*On*" 53). This "hermeneutic bootstrapping" grants the Foucauldian assumption that a regime of reading constitutes a text's meanings, framings, or interpretations, but situates the regimes within the text, making them a textual effect. In other words, neither texts and readers nor readers and regimes have an independent status or character; rather, their status and character depend on the regime of reading that constructs their relationship. As Frow says, "We are ourselves always positioned" ("*On*" 52).

CONCLUSION

Contrary to Frow, who brings Derridean and Foucauldian theory together in this way, Herman Rapport argues that in *Positions* and other works Derrida rejects Foucauldian accounts of the subject. Derrida shows that, based on Althusser's distinction of science and ideology, these accounts of "subject-position" reveal a "metaphysics of presence and absence" (80). I have already noted, however, that Bennett and Frow reject that Althusserian distinction. So do Macherey and Rancière.

Derrida also objects, Rapport says, that these accounts preserve "an essential mechanism" of "speculative Hegelian dialectics": "The position-of-the-other, in Hegelian dialectics, is always, finally to pose-oneself by oneself as . . . other-than-oneself in one's finite determination, with the aim of repatriating and reappropriating oneself, of returning close to oneself in the infinite richness of one's determination, etc." (96). I have argued, however, that not only Adorno, Heidegger, and Derrida but also Foucault repudiate the totalizing Hegelian practices whereby the differences of the other are transcended and the unity of the subject, what Rappaport terms the "repatriating and reappropriating oneself," is preserved. I have also suggested that their critiques not only of Hegelian dialectics but of instrumental or technological reason or the onto-theological tradition generate an antinomy between aesthetic critique and sociohistorical determination, an antinomy also evident in the cultural theory of Iser, Jauss, Fish, Mailloux, Macherey, Ranciére, Bennett, Frow, and others influenced by Adorno, Heidegger, or Foucault. That is, while Iser and Jauss grant reading or the reader an important place in interpretive practices, in Adorno's and Heidegger's fashion, Iser and, to an extent, Jauss defend the aesthetic autonomy and negativity of art not because art reveals the oppressive character of instrumental or equipmental reason and projects a utopian vision but because the transformative powers of aesthetic theory foster a dialog of author and reader or reveal a nonessentialist human plasticity. By contrast, like Fish and Mailloux, who reject the Heideggerian faith in aesthetics and opposition to instrumental reason and reveal the positive professional or rhetorical contexts of interpretive practices, Bennett, Macherey, and Rancière examine the positive history and influence of cultural institutions but, instead of preserving their speculative character, defend their normative force and situate them in their evolving historical context. The exception is Frow, whose account of what he calls "regimes of reading" moves beyond this opposition of aesthetics and cultural institutions. His textual, Derridean hermeneutics preserves the aesthetic negativity of Heideggerian aesthetics, especially its ability to affirm and undermine a text's interpretations, as well as the sociohistorical character of texts and readers or of regimes, communities, or reading formations regulating them.

In the remaining chapters studies of canonical and noncanonical British and American works including *Frankenstein*, Sara Paretsky's detective fiction, *Native Son, Light in August, Jazz*, and *The Adventures of Huckleberry Finn* will illustrate and clarify this Foucauldian account of cultural institutions' influence and history. These studies trace the varied receptions of those works to the American reader's changing cultural traditions and institutional contexts, which include the emergence of college-educated, female readers; the increasing influence of the media and higher education; the sciences' domination of educational institutions; the growth of women's, black, ethnic and other programs and movements; and the shifting status and conventions of popular mysteries, science fiction, and realist, naturalist, modernist, and postmodernist fiction.

GOTHIC ROMANCES AND THE MODERN HUMANITIES

THE CHANGING STATUS OF MARY SHELLEY'S *FRANKENSTEIN*

Frankenstein is an immature production, overburdened with literary baggage, by a gifted young person living in literate company. The monster is an unassimilated amalgam of bookish ogres: Caliban, Milton's Satan, travel-book giants. The novel cannot make up its mind whether this creature is an obscene freak or a lonely and generous savage with a cruelly unrequited yearning for love. The book is, in parallel ways, politically confused in its view of conquered peoples. That it laid itself open to vulgar adaptations onstage and elsewhere should not be put at Mary Shelley's door.

Claude Rawson
New York Times Book Review, p. 11
October 11, 2001

ONE OF THE CULTURAL INSTITUTIONS THAT FOUCAULDIAN reception study takes to explain a work's reception is the experimental sciences, whose vast expansion and enhanced influence after World War II moved American criticism to question the traditional assumption that the mad scientists, terrible monsters, divided selves, innocent victims, decaying castles, and other conventions made gothic horror fiction a minor genre. The revaluation of *Frankenstein* illustrates this change.

Like Claude Rawson, critics had described it as an improbable, immoral, disunified story with a didactic style and heretical views and Mary Shelley an uncreative writer, an irresponsible mother, and a clinging, sycophantic wife.[1] Since the 1970s critics have, by contrast, found Mary Shelley original, insightful, and critical, and the novel, rich, meaningful, and irreducible. In the anthology that began the new appreciation of the novel, George Levine and U. C. Knoepflmacher call it "both inexhaustible and inexplicable."[2]

To account for this revaluation, which produced many new interpretations as well as new editions, imitations, Web sites, movie versions, and classroom uses, Stephen Marcus says that "Mary Shelley seems to have been exceptionally responsive to reports of new experiments with electricity and in chemistry" (Marcus 200).[3] Other critics suggest that the novel's new value stems from what Schoene-Harwood terms "its radical indeterminacy and ambivalence, that is, its textual 'monstrosity.'"[4] Of course, Shelley's responsiveness to science's threats or the text's "monstrosity" do justify the novel's high value, but they do not explain why it was not until the 1970s that the novel gained this new value. What explains this revaluation is important changes in the social and cultural contexts governing early nineteenth-century British and mid-twentieth-century American reading practices. To summarize these changes briefly, while the nineteenth-century British critics who devalued the novel feared that the popularity of novels as well as their growing mass public and female readership threatened to undermine the aristocratic social order, the modern American critics who revalue the novel challenge the marginal status to which the natural sciences reduced the humanities in mid-twentieth-century America.[5]

THE NINETEENTH-CENTURY RECEPTION OF THE NOVEL

Although the novel has been ranked as high art since the 1970s, when the sciences had already imposed their hegemony, initially, the critical reception of *Frankenstein* was very negative. Of eleven reviews written between 1818 and 1833, eight were mixed (3) or negative (5). Only three were positive, and two of them were written by Percy Bysse Shelley, Mary Shelley's husband, and Sir Walter Scott, her editor's choice.

Sir Walter Scott's positive review anticipates the novel's modern classification as science fiction. He described it as a "marvelous romance" of the sort in which "the author has deduced, in the course of his narrative, the probable consequences of the possession" of scientific secrets "upon the fortunes and mind of him who might enjoy them" (Scott 42).[6] By contrast, the negative reviewers faulted her imagination, theories, and gender. Some complained that Shelley's "diseased and wandering imagination . . . has stepped out of all legitimate bounds" (Anon. April 1818) or that her "wild and irregular theories" violated "our established and most sacred notions" (Hunter 191–96). Others fault her sex as well as her "wild" theories and "diseased imagination." As a reviewer for *The British Critic* said,

There are occasional symptoms of no common powers of mind, struggling through a mass of absurdity, which well nigh overwhelms them; but it is a sort of absurdity that approaches so often the confines of what is wicked and immoral, that we dare hardly trust ourselves to bestow even this qualified praise. The writer of it is, we understand, a female; this is an aggravation of that which is the prevailing fault of the novel; but if our authoress can forget the gentleness of her sex, it is no reason why we should; and we shall therefore dismiss the novel without further comment. (April 1818)

Still others objected that *Frankenstein* was "piously dedicated" to William Godwin, the philosophical Jacobin whose "literary family . . . strangely delights in . . . the most afflicting and humiliating of human miseries" (Hunter 198).

Although twentieth-century critics also fault Shelley's style or femininity, these critics do not share the reviewers' hostility to her Godwinian radicalism.[7] In the 1832 edition Mary Shelley takes a more conservative stance, but not in the 1818 edition, which openly declares her radicalism. Not only does she dedicate the novel to her father William Godwin, whose philosophical Jacobinism was roundly condemned as monstrous, she also made the novel parallel to his *Caleb Williams*.

How extensive are the parallels between *Frankenstein* and *Caleb Williams*? As several critics have noted, both novels show that human virtue and social justice break down in the face of physically or morally monstrous characters (see Clifford and Harvey). Unlike Frankenstein, Williams serves as the assistant of Falkland, his noble patron, but Frankenstein and Williams both grow up in well-to-do families and freely pursue their intellectual interests. Williams studies Greek and Roman literature, while Frankenstein devotes himself to alchemy and, after traveling to Ingolstadt, to chemistry. With classical allusions and other learned devices, Williams obsessively seeks the secret of Falkland's moody and withdrawn state, so much so that, in order to confirm his suspicion that

Falkland is a murderer, he neglects his duties and well-being and brings on Falkland's wrath. Similarly, Frankenstein neglects his family, his health, and nature's beauties in an equally obsessive pursuit of life's secrets. As a result, he gives life to a creature whose ugliness subsequently appalls and disillusions him and whose anger eventually destroys him, his friend Clerval, and his family. Williams speaks of living in oppression and misery because of his foe; when Frankenstein realizes that the creature killed his brother William, he too complains that he lives in oppression and misery: "I bore a hell within me, which nothing could extinguish" (57). After the trial at which Williams, framed by Falkland, is unjustly convicted of robbery and sent to prison, Williams considers humans brutal monsters. After the trial at which Justine, framed by the creature, is unjustly convicted of murdering William and sentenced to death, Elizabeth also considers men "monsters thirsting for each other's blood" (61), and Frankenstein laments "the fiend lurking in his heart" (61).

More importantly, educated by themselves and suffering from bad "fathers," Williams and the creature parallel each other. They both feel that society has turned against them and excludes and persecutes them unjustly. While the creature's monstrous appearance explains his persecution, the ubiquitous Gines, whom Falkland hired to spy on and expose him, and the media, which sells the "WONDERFUL AND SUPRISING HISTORY OF CALEB WILLIAMS" throughout the country, explain his. In addition, to escape the persecution, they both conceal themselves. Williams disguises himself as a beggar, a Jew, and a handicapped person and moves to various towns, where he makes new friends, including Laura, a self-taught scholar. Similarly, hiding in a shed, the creature befriends the De Lacey family, observing and helping them secretly and learning from them how to speak and to read. Although Laura welcomes Williams into her family, when she learns of his reputation as an evil person, she abruptly excludes him because he is, she says, "a monster and not a man" (348), and he becomes very distraught: "I felt a sudden torpor and sickness that pervaded every fiber of my frame" (349). When the creature introduces himself to the blind old father, Felix the son throws him out of their cabin. They flee from him, and he rages in anguish, burning down their abandoned cabin. At the end, to revenge himself on Falkland, Williams convinces a magistrate to arrange a hearing to charge Falkland with murder, but at the hearing Falkland looks so terribly sick and weak that Williams reverses himself, praising Falkland's character and wishing himself dead. Similarly, to revenge himself, the creature kills William, Clerval, and Elizabeth, and frames Justine, but at the end the creature too reverses himself: weeping, he blames himself for Frankenstein's death and condemns himself to death.

These parallels emphasize the Godwinian disillusionment whereby the obsessions of the characters produce monstrosities subverting human virtue and social justice. At the same time, the parallels break down, undermining the disillusionment. For example, to explain his anger and violence, the creature says that he was abandoned by his "father" Frankenstein and that humans, terrified by his monstrosity, exclude him from their society. Similarly, Williams blames Falkland and his aristocratic society for his suffering. What breaks the parallel is that, after Frankenstein destroys the unfinished body of the creature's female companion, Frankenstein accepts his own responsibility for human suffering: "I shuddered to think that future ages might curse me as their pest, whose selfishness had not hesitated to buy its own peace at the price perhaps of the existence of the whole human race" (115).

While *Caleb Williams* and *Frankenstein* both show that human virtue and social justice reveal monstrous brutality and intolerance, Frankenstein's character develops beyond this Godwinian disillusionment. So do *Frankenstein's* interpellated narratives. In *Caleb Williams*, the interprellated narrative of Collins, Falkland's trusted servant, describes Falkland's withdrawal from social life and justifies Williams's belief that Falkland is a murderer. By contrast, the narratives of Walton, Frankenstein, and the creature do not fit together very neatly. In the letters addressed to his sister Mrs. Saville, Walton explains that he travels to the North Pole to satisfy a youthful desire for scientific discovery. Frankenstein says that in his youth, he showed a comparable enthusiasm for alchemy and for chemistry. He too imagined his discovering how to create life would benefit humanity, but the dream in which, as he embraces Elizabeth, she turns into his dead mother suggests that his scientific experiment expresses a repressed desire to restore his dead mother, rather than a benevolent wish to improve human life. Moreover, his success in producing the creature turns him against science because it destroys him, his father, Clerval, Elizabeth, and Williams.

The more positive narrative of the creature implicitly adopts the trial and error methods of a dispassionate scientist. When, for example, he first enters the forest, he avoids what hurts him and seeks out what pleases him: "How strange, I thought, that the same cause should produce such opposite effects" (69). When they meet for the first time, an enraged Victor threatens to kill him: "Begone, vile insect! Or rather stay that I may trample you to dust" (65), whereas he calmly explains the causes of his violence.

In addition to science's status, the narratives contrast the gender roles of the Frankenstein and De Lacey families. For example, just as Carolyn Beaufort marries Alphonse because she feels so grateful that he assisted her and her impoverished father, so Victor feels so closely bound to the family that he can form no new attachments when he leaves it, and he readily agrees to his dying mother's request that he marry his cousin (or adopted sister) Elizabeth. The De Lacey family is also bound closely together, but, unlike Elizabeth, who devotes herself to the family, Safie travels on her own to Switzerland, where the De Laceys have been exiled and where, contrary to her father's wish, she joins Felix (see Mellor "Possessing" 477).

While, as I will show, the critics who revalued the novel attribute profound significance to these contrasting narratives, the negative reviews and criticism harshly critique the novel's Godwinian realism. These opposed evaluations imply that the sociocultural contexts regulating reading practices have changed sharply since the late eighteenth century. As scholars have suggested, at that time the growth of a newly literate, mass English reading audience and the commercial production of English novels, especially the popular gothic horror story, generated intense conservative anxieties. In the late eighteenth and early nineteenth centuries, circulating libraries, steam printing, and new technologies made cheap newspapers, magazines, tracts, serials, and editions more widely available. The growth of commerce and trade, which gave the middle classes more leisure for reading, and of mass literacy, which Sunday Schools, charity schools, adult mechanics institutes, and other institutions succeeded in producing, aroused conservative fears that these new reading habits could undermine the established social order as radically as the French revolution had.[8] Opposing the widespread popularity of novels, especially gothic romances, and their increasingly private consumption, critics feared that these novels exercised a dangerously seductive influence on their female readers in particular. Instead of reading them in a family or public context, the female readers consumed them privately and experienced an illicit sensual pleasure.[9]

The critics regretted that, unlike more positive or wholesome literature, which men read aloud in a family setting while the children would listen and the women would sew or perform some other domestic duty, women read such novels privately, consuming them like food and feeling an improper sensual delight.[10]

Mary Shelley challenged this debased view of novels and defended their readers. Like Shelley, who was self-educated, the monster teaches himself to read and thereby represents both the democratic aspirations of women and the working class and also conservative fears of their monstrosity.[11] In *Northanger Abbey*, which was also written by a British woman and published in 1818, Jane Austen too challenged this debased view of novels and their readers. In an ambiguous manner, Catherine's suspicions of the Abbey and General Tilney reveal the dangerous consequences of the Gothic romances, yet the narrator intervenes to defend novels and their readers: "I will not adopt that ungenerous and impolitic custom so common with novel-writers, of degrading by their contemptuous censure the very performances, to the number of which they are themselves adding" (29).[12]

In addition, this novel also rejects the conventions of gothic romances, in which, the narrator tells us, "human nature, at least in the Midland Counties of England, was" not "to be looked for" (166), and describes her heroine's ordinary life and psychological development. With monstrous characters who, like Isabella or General Tilney, calculate the financial gains resulting from their human relationships, the novel also realistically represents the terrible evils described by the gothic romances. As the narrator says of her heroine Catherine, "[I]n suspecting General Tilney of either murdering or shutting up his wife, she had scarcely sinned against his character, or magnified his cruelty" (207).

The histories of the two novels have, nonetheless, been remarkably different. Published posthumously, *Northanger Abbey* may have found readers among those who patronized British lending libraries,[13] but, like her other novels, it was not financially successful, not until the 1870s, when Austen's nephew Austen-Leigh wrote a popular biography of her. What earned her novels high status was not commercial success but the influence of powerful Victorian liberals like Thomas Babington MacCauley, who called Austen the Shakespeare of English prose, and John Henry Lewes, who considered her and Fielding "the greatest novelists in our language."[14] As the Victorian writer Mrs. Oliphant points out, the liberals turned the work of Austen into classical fiction with which it became "the duty of every student of recent English literature to be more or less acquainted . . . 'The best judges' have here done the office of an Academy."[15] While *Frankenstein* was, at best, classified as science fiction or, at worst, called "a tissue of horrible and disgusting absurdity" (Croker 189), Austen's fiction acquired the status of classical literature with which it was "the duty of every student of recent English literature to be more or less acquainted," and good "Aunt Jane" was described as a withdrawn, religious woman humbly but accurately chronicling the customs of eighteenth-century rural England.

What made *Frankenstein* successful was not the opinion of the "best judges" but its many nineteenth-century theatrical productions and its twentieth-century film and television versions, which rejected the novel's realistic depiction of science and reinstated the horror story's gothic conventions, including Fritz, the laboratory assistant who explains the story and carries out Frankenstein's directions; the intimidating gothic castle at the top of which a mature Frankenstein has constructed a giant laboratory; and an inarticulate monster genetically programmed for violence.[16] A reviewer of *Presumption*, a popular 1823 theatrical production, aptly summarized the results: "In the novel the rigid moralist may feel himself constantly offended, by the modes of reasoning, principles of action, &c. But in the Drama this is all carefully kept in the background. Nothing but what can please, astonish, and delight, is there suffered to appear."[17] The novel rejects the conventions of gothic fiction and critiques scientific rationality and social justice in Godwin's realist fashion only to receive harsh criticism from most reviewers and many nineteenth- and twentieth-century critics, while the play and film versions reinstate the gothic conventions, making the story a popular depiction of destructive technoscience.[18]

In the early nineteenth century, critics faulted popular novels because novels were not a legitimate genre and because the mass reading public as well as the many female novel readers threatened the aristocratic social and intellectual order. By the mid-twentieth century, the novel had become a well-respected genre, and mass public and higher education had been widely accepted. At this time, what aroused conservative fears was not the growth of female, working-class, or minority readers but the domination of the natural sciences.

After modern literary criticism achieved professional autonomy in the 1930s and 1940s and went on to acquire diverse schools and movements in the 1960s, the sciences came to dominate both secondary and higher education. At that time, vast new government funding gave the experimental sciences what Hugh Graham and Nancy Diamond call a golden age: "The golden age in federal funding of academic research was the post-Sputnik decade, 1958–68. In that span, federal R&D funding for universities jumped from $254 million to $1.57 billion, an increase of 618 percent" (Graham and Diamond 47).

C. P. Snow's *The Two Cultures*, published in 1964, caused so much unexpected controversy because Snow praised the new power of the sciences and labeled the humanists Luddites ignorant of and antagonistic to the sciences (17). It is well-known that F. R. Leavis, Lionel Trilling, and other leading humanists sharply criticized Snow's view. Less familiar is the response of George Levine, whose 1979 anthology initiated the revaluation of *Frankenstein*. In *The Scientist vs the Humanist* (1963), he and Owen Thomas maintain that the controversy over the two cultures represents "the longstanding antagonism between those who see the meaning of life in terms of material progress and increased knowledge of the natural world and those who see it only in the personal fulfillment of every man's 'humanity'—of his moral, intellectual, and aesthetic capacities" (Levine and Thomas vii). Opposing Snow, this "longstanding antagonism" clearly sets the morality and aesthetics of the humanities above "the material progress" and "increased knowledge" of science.

My reader might object that the ones initiating the revaluation of *Frankenstein* were not just humanists who opposed the science's domination but also feminists who interpreted *Frankenstein* in terms of women's experience of patriarchy, family, and childbirth.[19] It is true that in the 1970s, when feminism was establishing itself in academia, feminist scholars constructed a female literary tradition that made the novel a precursor or "foremother" of modern women's literature;[20] nonetheless, these scholars also opposed the scientific practices of feminist biology or sociology.[21]

My reader may also object that *Frankenstein* is valuable because it shows man's unconscious desires or dramatizes irreconcilable views of human life, not because it depicts science's evil consequences. For example, Levine, who takes Victor to contain not only the monster but Clerval and Walton as well and Justine to be part of Elizabeth, claims that this doubling of the characters shows that the novel explores irrational or incestuous desires (Levine 208–13). Lawrence

Lipking grants that in the realist fashion *Frankenstein* faults the ambition of the overreaching scientist, as Levine says, but goes on to argue that in the romantic manner the novel makes claims about man, nature, society, and God that invariably deconstruct themselves or devolve into the contrary or opposite views (Lipking 319–20). Similarly, Fred Botting argues that, since the "many oppositions in *Frankenstein* do not sustain a unified set of meanings" (Botting 47), the text always eludes readings that seek to fix and to master it in Frankenstein's manner: "Reading becomes a matter of the construction and exclusion of text-monsters at the same time that it repeats the desire for presence or imaginary mastery" (Botting 17). Botting is right to suggest that to reduce the novel to a critique of science would to repeat "the desire for presence or imaginary mastery; however, the irreducible text does not exclude such a reading either, for the formal devices or aesthetic irreducibility of the text both allow and undermine not only the evil consequences which readers attribute to science but also the terrible monsters, divided selves, innocent victims, decaying castles, and other generic devices in terms of which readers traditionally explain science fiction or gothic horror stories.

Other critics grant that the novel undermines the domination of science and the formulaic genres of popular culture but argue that the novel's value lies not in this subversive import but in what Schoene-Harwood terms "its radical indeterminacy and ambivalence, that is, its textual 'monstrosity'" (Schoene-Harwood 8; see also Botting 3–4). Patrick Brantlinger claims, for example, that, as I suggested, Shelley's creature represents the "monstrosity" of self-educated, nineteenth-century female and working-class readers. He also claims, however, that, itself a monstrosity, the novel shows "an uncontrollable, irrational excess of signification that transcends the boundaries of normal, comprehensible discourse"

(Brantlinger 59; see also Gard 24; Lipking 319–20). In other words, he construes the novel in contrary terms, with its "monstrous" nineteenth-century working class and female readers as its local, historical context and the monstrous or irreducible Derridean "excess of signification" as the novel's universal truth.

In other words, *Frankenstein* has become a monstrosity not because the text always exceeds any account of its meaning or because Shelley insightfully identified the dangers of gothic horror stories or experimental science but because the greatly enhanced influence of the modern sciences has moved Anglo-American humanists to appreciate the novel in new and important ways. In the next chapter, I will suggest that the integration of American public and higher education and the growth of black studies have led critics to reevaluate *The Adventures of Huckleberry Finn* in a similar way. First, however, I should enquire whether or not the new appreciation of *Frankenstein* successfully resists the domination of the sciences and restores the centrality of the humanities. Does not the continuing influence and prestige of the sciences render such resistance self-defeating? May not the modern critics who have discovered the insight or irreducibility of high art in this nineteenth-century gothic romance only be digging a deeper hole for the humanities? As Cathy Davidson and David Goldberg say, "The prevailingly antagonistic stance within the humanities toward science and technology" is "also partly to blame" for the humanities' marginal status (53).

CHAPTER 4

THE ADVENTURES OF HUCKLEBERRY FINN

FROM LIBERAL REALISM TO MULTICULTURALISM

BECAUSE THE SCIENCES HAVE DOMINATED AMERICAN universities since the 1960s, Anglo-American readers were moved to appreciate *Frankenstein* in new and important ways. More dramatically, the integration of American public and higher education has sparked dramatic reevaluations of *The Adventures of Huckleberry Finn*. Since American public and higher education was integrated in the 1960s and 1970s, this well-established classic, which is taught in more schools than any other literary work except Shakespeare's plays (Arac 7), provoked new controversies in academic circles as well as in public schools.

In 2000 the PBS program *Culture Shock* reported, for example, that in Tempe, Arizona, Kathy Monteiro campaigned to remove *Huckleberry Finn* from her teenage daughter's high school curriculum. As she explained, "I'm wondering as a teacher and as a mother, how you can ask kids to go home and read the word 'nigger' 200-something times . . . and then expect kids to come back to school and not use the word" ("Born to Trouble"). Such complaints have some justification. Not only do Huck, Pap, and others use the term "nigger" 213 times, but also in the minstrel fashion Twain depicts Jim and other blacks as darkies or as childlike, and, as a result, promotes white supremacy or, at the least, bad racial relations. On the other hand, the novel satirizes the characters who reveal racist attitudes. Indeed, since Jim was good to Huck and devoted to his family, and since Huck decides to go to hell rather than turn Jim in or let him return to slavery, the novel resists Southern racism.

In a recent edition, Gerald Graff and James Phelan examine these contrary interpretations of the novel, presenting excerpts that defend both sides and emphasizing the pedagogical value that classroom discussions of the controversy can have. Graff and Phelan say little, if anything, however, about the novel's reception. What explains why the novel has such contrary meanings? What explains the controversy?

I will argue that the roots of the controversy are in the nineteenth century, when reviewers and critics took the novel to represent a Dickensian realism that allows both the conservative affirmation and the liberal critique of the Antebellum South. In a Dickensian manner, the novel preserves the integrity of the South's middle-class community but satirizes not only the racism of the South but also its aristocratic ethos, religious fundamentalism, middle-class virtues, British cultural ideals, and so on. The Dickensian character of its realism was lost in the early twentieth century, when Twain acquired the reputation of a genuine American personality and *Huckleberry Finn* the status of a great American novel. In the 1960s, when, because of higher education's vast growth, academic criticism displaced middlebrow journals as the arbiters of literary values, the racial aspects of the novel became controversial. Not only did its readers include the blacks and minorities in the newly integrated American schools; in addition, the black cultural movements established in the 1960s and 1970s justified reevaluations of the novel, including reinterpretions of Jim's character.

Some critics argue, by contrast, that the controversy begins not in the 1890s, with Dickensian realism, but in the 1930s and 1940s, when cold-war liberals opposed Harriet Beecher Stowe's or Richard Wright's "sentimental" protest fiction (see Arac). Other critics grant that the "cultural conversation" began the 1890s but minimize the controversy on the grounds that the reader sees through stock phrases and ideological discourses and grasps Twain's ironic or satirical ends (see Mailloux, *Power*). My argument is not only that the controversy began in the 1890s but also that the controversy matters because the character of the reader has changed markedly since then.

TWAIN'S DICKENSIAN REALISM

Huckleberry Finn employs a first-person narration in which Huck speaks in dialect, whereas in *Oliver Twist* the third-person narrator has limited omniscience, and, despite his impoverished upbringing, Oliver always speaks in proper English; nonetheless, *Huckleberry Finn* and *Oliver Twist* reveal parallels that clarify *Huckleberry Finn*'s Dickensian realism. For example, both works satirize the middle-class figures who unjustly oppress the youthful protagonist. The well-known scene in which Oliver, a hungry orphan living in the workhouse, asks for more food produces much satire of Mr. Bumble the beadle and the workhouse board, which, because of his request, consider him a lost soul given over to the Devil. As the old gentleman says, "I know that boy will be hung" (58). Similarly, when the Widow Douglass and Miss Watson try to civilize Huck, their efforts are also satirized because they too fear that he will end up in hell and because, unlike the hungry Oliver, who suffers virtuously but silently, Huck faults and deceives them.

Similarly, when Pap learns that, because of the robbers captured in *The Adventures of Tom Sawyer*, Huck acquired substantial funds and entrusted them to Judge Thatcher to invest for him, Pap kidnaps Huck, locking him in a cabin hidden along the river and trying to "make the law" give him the money. Although Oliver's brother Monk is more devious than Pap, he too contrives to obtain Oliver's funds, but he means to destroy any evidence of Oliver's family lineage or any form of his moral virtue.

After the workhouse board apprentices Oliver to Sowerberry the undertaker, Oliver beats his fellow apprentice Noah Claypool for insulting his dead mother and is beaten, in turn, by the whole family, who lock him up in the cellar. This beating is also satirized when, for example, Bumble blames Oliver's fighting on his being too well fed (93) or Mrs. Sowerberry exclaims, "Oh! . . . What a mercy we had not all been murdered in our bed" (90). The beating produces pathos as well because, alone in the cellar, Oliver, "hiding his face in his hands, wept such tears as . . . few so young may ever have cause to weep before him" (95). After a drunken Pap, seeing snakes and ghosts, pulls out a knife and tries to kill Huck, he also escapes from his confinement; however, in Twain's hard-boiled manner Huck fools Pap and the townspeople into thinking he has been killed and on Jackson's Island watches them search for his dead body while he eats the bread they float on the river to find it.

Unlike *Huckleberry Finn*, *Oliver Twist* is sentimental; still, both novels satirize oppressive figures of authority. Moreover, in both novels, the protagonist undertakes a journey that brings him into contact with individuals, both good and evil, who represent diverse aspects of social life. Hungry, penniless, and alone, Oliver walks to London, where he meets the Jewish Fagin and joins his gang of thieves. He also joins the middle-class household of the benevolent Mr. Brownlow and Rose Maylie. More independent and resourceful, Huck, together with the escaping Jim, finds a comfortable raft and floats down the Mississippi River, pilfering food from passing farms and enjoying the good life. In the process, Huck encounters various problematic individuals, including the Shepherdsons, who represent the South's aristocratic code of honor, the boatsmen who, in the excised raft chapter, tell the tall tales characteristic of the West, and the Duke and King, who are typical embezzlers.

Oliver's inherent repugnance to evil moves him to flee when the Artful Dodger tries to steal Mr. Brownlow's handkerchief or to resist when Bill Sikes tries to rob the home of the Giles. This resistance turns Fagin and Sikes against him but earns him the goodwill of Brownlow and Maylie, who eventually establish his true family ties and restore him to their middle-class community.

Huck and Jim are also forced to accommodate the Duke and the King, who come onto the raft to escape punishment by angry mobs; however, when the farmer who buys Jim turns out to be Silas Phelps, the uncle of Tom Sawyer, Huck is also restored to his middle-class community and feels equally delighted; as he says, "It was like being born again" (293). Moreover, just as the will of Oliver's father returns him to his family and community, so the will of Miss Watson, not Tom's evasion and bungled escape, frees Jim to recover his family and join the community. The difference is that, when Oliver learns that Rose and Mrs. Maylie are his close relations, he lets the tears fall. As the narrator says, "joy and grief were mingled in the cup" (463). By contrast, Huck's joy fades when at the end he learns that Aunt Sally intends to adopt and civilize him. Then he plans to "light out for the Territory" because he "can't stand it" (369).

In short, both works satirize oppressive figures of authority and in their protagonists' journeys depict figures representing the diverse aspects of social life. Moreover, each depicts a reversal in which, thanks to middle-class generosity and goodness, the protagonist preserves his virtue and in the end rejoins his middle-class community. With Mr. Brownlow's recollections of Oliver's parents and Monk's opposition to his inheritance, Dickens is careful to prepare the reader for the reversal of Oliver's fortunes; by contrast, the reversal of Huck's and Jim's fortunes surprises the reader. As his friend and critic William D. Howells explains, Twain "would take whatever offered itself to his hand . . . and leave the reader to look after relevancies and sequences for himself" (53). In other words, Twain repudiates the sentimentality of Dickens but preserves the liberal satire and with the surprising reversal the conservative affirmation of the community.

Construed in its own or in Twain's terms, rather than those of nineteenth-century realism, the novel emphasizes the moral development of Huck, not his experience of typical characters nor the reversal reintegrating him into the community. In this version, the novel begins where *The Adventures of Tom Sawyer* left off: As Huck says, "You don't know about me without you have read" *Tom Sawyer*, which ends after Tom and Huck acquire substantial funds from the robbery that they have uncovered (49). Huck entrusted his funds to Judge Thatcher, who invests them for him, but, when he suspects that Pap, thought dead, has come back, he sells them to the judge for a dollar. When Pap learns about these funds, he kidnaps Huck, locking him in a cabin hidden along the river. In a satirical moment, he rails against the "govment" and a free "mulatter" but falls over a tub of salt pork and, in anger, kicks it only to smash up his exposed toe.

The novel does not break with this storyline until Huck meets the escaping Jim on Jackson's Island and together they float down the Mississippi River, pilfering food from passing farms and enjoying the good life. In the process, Huck undergoes a moral education. For instance, the feud of the Shepherdsons and the Grangerfords teaches him about the South's aristocratic codes. In the excised raft chapter, the tall tales of the boatsmen teach him about Western humor. The embezzling Duke and King teach him how easily religious sentimentality can be exploited.

More importantly, when Jim faults his account of "Sollermun," or when in the raft episode Jim makes him apologize, Huck learns to appreciate Jim's humanity. After the king sells Jim back into slavery, Huck at first decides to write to Miss Watson to tell her where she can find Jim, but, after he remembers how good Jim was to him, he decides that he will free Jim and accept his punishment in hell. This decision shows that the trip down the Mississippi has brought about his moral improvement; however, when he discovers, to his surprise, that Tom is willing to help him, he accepts Tom's insistence that the escape proceed in keeping with the romantic escapes described in "the books." In other words, Twain shows Huck breaking with Southern racism and recognizing Jim's humanity but unable to sustain this moral insight, which collapses into farce when at the end Jim suffers from snakes, spiders, and other torments and, when he is recaptured, is bound in chains and nearly lynched.

This account explains Huck's development as well as his limits, but the account assumes that Huck's point of view adequately explains his relationship with Jim. A third account, based on black history, slave narratives, and black literature, argues that Huck does not recognize the complexity of Jim. In several episodes Jim, showing his independence, challenges Huck. For example, in the raft episode, Jim accuses Huck of treating him like trash, and Huck brings himself to apologize to a "nigger." Huck is not so humble, though, when Jim faults "Sollermun" for having a harem ["would a wise man want to live in de mids' er such a blimblammin' all de time?" (133)] and for choosing a poor way to determine which woman the baby really belonged to. These arguments also show Jim's independence but bring out Huck's feelings of supremacy: "You can't learn a nigger to argue" (136). In other episodes, Jim accepts Huck's feelings of supremacy and acts as the childish darkie of the minstrel tradition beloved by Twain. For instance, Jim goes along with Tom's humiliating evasion, putting up with snakes, spiders, and other torments and, to save Tom, risking recapture, because only Tom and Huck offer him hope of escape. In other words, despite Twain's racist attitudes, Jim's experiences reveal what an escaped slave had to do to survive in the Old South.

THE RECEPTION OF *HUCKLEBERRY FINN*

As Dickensian realism, Twain's art, and African American experience, the novel presents contrary versions that reveal the historical differences between contemporary and late nineteenth-century literary study. In the late nineteenth century, while universities, which were changing into research institutions, taught the rhetoric of the Greek and Roman classics, middlebrow magazines like the *Atlantic Monthly* conferred literary value on contemporary American fiction. In the 1860s the magazines that Nancy Glazener terms the "Atlanta group," which published many of the novel's reviews, promoted the literary realism of Dickens, Thackeray, and other British writers (37), but by the 1880s they favored an American realism that constructed "realist authorship as professional authorship" and "sensational and sentimental authorship" as unprofessional (13). Considered manly, this professional realism opposed the sentimental fiction not only of Dickens but also of Susan Ashton-Warner, Harriet Beecher Stowe, and other female American writers, whose works were flooding the markets at that time (see Douglass 8).

Some reviewers of *Huckleberry Finn* complained that it lacked a moral and with its humor sought only commercial success; other reviewers promoted this manly American realism because it depicted the customs and manners and the typical characters of the Southeast. Branders Matthews said, for example, that "the chief players in the present drama . . . are taken from life, no doubt, but they are so aptly chosen and so broadly drawn that they are quite as typical as they are actual" (Budd, *Reviews* 262). Other reviewers said that "Mr. Clemens describes things as they really were, in Missouri" (Budd, *Reviews* 267), that the novel is a "minute and faithful picture of Southwestern manners and customs fifty years ago" (Budd, *Reviews* 270), and that "any one who has ever lived in the Southwest, or who has visited that section, will recognize the truth of all these sketches and the art with which they are brought into this story" (Budd, *Reviews* 272; see also 276, 278, and 280).

These reviews praise the novel's accurate detail and representative characters and settings, two of nineteenth-century realism's key aspects, according to Donald Pizer (263–64); however, instead of commending its "idealistic view of human nature," realism's third key aspect, the reviewers praise the novel's satirical humor: "the most amusing book Mark Twain has written for years" (274). For instance, in his 1901 essay, William Dean Howells, who was Twain's friend and advisor, commends the novel's remarkable humor but attributes it to Twain's "consciousness of the grotesque absurdities in the Southern inversion of the civilized ideals" (57).

Howells claims that Twain's southern origins make possible not only his humor but also his realism. "The strict religiosity compatible in the Southwest with savage precepts of conduct is something that could make itself known in its amusing contrast only to the native" (57). What also explains his comic realism is, however, the influential fiction of Charles Dickens, who was extraordinarily popular in the nineteenth century. Despite repeated denials, Twain carefully and constantly read Dickens for over fifty years (see Gardner 191). Called the American Dickens (see Gair 143), Twain followed the example of Bret Harte, who, influence by Dickens, sympathetically depicted whores, gamblers, miners, and highway robbers, thereby extending the range of American fiction. Twain was disgusted by the "slavish" imitation of Dickens (Baetzhold 306; see also 194), yet, as Walter Blair points out, "Twain, eager for acceptance by the literary elite, hardly would have ventured to make Huck the center of a novel if the trail had not been broken by Harte" (113). As Twain put it, Harte, Twain's close friend and literary mentor in the mid-1860s, "trimmed and trained and schooled me patiently until he changed me from an awkward utterer of coarse grotesqueness to a writer of paragraphs and chapters that have found favor in the eyes of even some of the very decentest people in the land" (cited in Nissen 86). In 1877, Twain renounced and condemned Harte, disgusted by his freeloading, his characters' sexuality, and, most importantly, his Dickensian pathos. As Twain wrote in 1906, "He hadn't a sincere fiber in him. I think he was incapable of emotion, for I think he had nothing to feel with. I think his heart was merely a pump and had no other function. . . . This is the very Bret Harte whose pathetics, imitated from Dickens, used to be a godsend to the farmers of two hemispheres on account of the freshets of tears they compelled" (Krauth 17–18).

Although Dickens and Harte influenced Twain, Howells denies that Twain's manly realism indulges any such Dickensian "pathetics": "[I]n the work of Mark Twain there is little of the pathos which is supposed to be the ally of humor, little suffusion of apt tears from the smiling eyes. It is too sincere for that sort of play" (56). Howells does not identify the pathos or apt tears with Dickens, Harte, or feminine sentimentality, but the distinction between humor suffused with pathos and humor that is "sincere" clearly divides Twain, whom Howells terms the "Westerner," from the European Dickens or Harte.

As American literature was established as an independent field, critics still esteemed the novel, but this distinction between feminine, Dickensian sentimentality and "sincere" humor gets lost because critics made Twain representative of America, not just the West. In 1912, two years after his death, Albert Paine, his first biographer, called him "the foremost American-born author—the man most characteristically American in every thought and word and action of his life" (112). In 1913, H. L. Mencken considered Twain "the true father of our national literature, the first genuinely American artist of the blood royal" (71) and *Huckleberry Finn* "one of the great masterpieces of the world" (71). After WWI, when Van Wyck Brooks challenged the high estimation of Twain, claiming that his true self was repressed and distorted by his commercial society and his self-righteous family, Bernard De Voto vindicated Twain's high reputation and American character, In a nationalist fashion he maintained, however, that, raised on Western folk tales, Twain felt little pressure from Europe's "damn shadow" (99).

Lionel Trilling and T. S. Eliot, who initiated what Jonathan Arac terms the novel's hypercanonization, extended this nationalist view, calling it the greatest American novel. They maintained, however, that Twain's mythical depiction of the river, not his realistic accounts of Missouri customs or typical characters, establishes its greatness. Eliot claimed, for example, that "the River makes the book a great book" because it reminds us of "the power and terror of Nature and the isolation and feebleness of Man" (48). Similarly, Huck's serving the "river-god," Trilling said, makes the novel "a great book" because it represents what he terms "moral realism" (*Liberal* 109). Giving the novel modernist features, Eliot and Trilling noted, in addition to the mythic River, parallels between Huck and Stephen Daedalus, who also seeks a lost father, and the novel's influence on Ernest Hemingway and others, who esteem its first-person narration. What's more, they too explicitly repudiate fiction of sentimentality, but it is the protest fiction or, as Eliot says, the "sensationalist propaganda" of Harriet Beecher Stowe or Richard Wright, not the sentimental realism of Dickens, that they reject. As Arac points out, in the 1940s and 1950s, when cold war anticommunism gained widespread influence, the sentimentality of *Uncle Tom's Cabin* was associated not so much with nineteenth-century British literature as with left-wing or procommunist protest fiction. Arac adds that in a modernist fashion Trilling finds *Huckleberry Finn* subversive because, unlike protest fiction, it resists what he termed the Stalinist conformity of the American middle class.

In the 1960s Leo Marx and Henry Nash Smith also reject sentimentality in this cold war fashion and esteem the novel's subversion of middle-class values. In Trilling's manner, they consider Huck and Jim morally autonomous characters resisting the corruptions of civilized life. As a result, they consider Huck's decision to free Jim and go to hell a heroic victory "over the prevailing morality" (57; see Smith 67–68), but they fault the conclusion, which reveals Twain's inability to escape from the genteel tradition. As Marx says, "he had nothing solid to put in its place" (58). More negative is Smith, who says that Twain's identification with Tom and not Huck at the end shows his recognition that "Huck and Jim's quest for freedom was only a dream" (74).

Marx and Smith's views of the conclusion's failure proved very controversial. Some critics rejected their view on the historical grounds that the conclusion forcefully satirizes the South's views of emancipation and reconstruction. These readings, which Arac terms allegorical because they lack textual justification, reassert the novel's satire of British sentimentality, including Sir Walter Scott's romantic "evasions" (see Nilon). Other accounts grant that Twain stereotypes Jim or allows Huck, Pap, and others racist views but, to defend the novel, argue that the characters' comic performance, mythic status, or Twain's irony or satire undermines them or, at least, mitigates their import (see Cox, "A Hard Book"). Such defenses preserve the novel's status as a modernist work divorced from political or social ends, precluding any treatment of it "as merely an instrument in the furtherance of the politics, religion, or morals it appears to recommend" (Donohue, *Classics* 245).

Other accounts argue that, while Twain rejected slavery, he could not consistently accept the humanity or equality of Jim, who is finally depicted in keeping with the minstrel tradition beloved by Twain (see Bell; Woodard and McCann). Still other critics say that, far from Jim's playing the childish darky or providing Huck the father that Pap never was, Jim and Huck need each other if they are to survive. Treating the novel as a lesson in black history, these readings say that Jim wears the masks that a typical slave needed to survive. Sometimes he challenges Huck's views, evoking Huck's white supremacist attitudes; other times, especially at the end, he plays the role of childish darky represented by the minstrel tradition because he needs the support of Huck and Tom (see Chadwick-Joshua and Robinson).

Arac argues that what explains these contrary interpretations is the "hypercanonization" of *Huckleberry Finn* produced by the cold war liberalism of Trilling, Marx, Smith, and others who made modernist nonconformity the paradigm of genuine political activity (31). This argument assumes that the critique of sentimentality began in the 1930s, when cold war liberals like Trilling repudiated the protest fiction of Wright or Stowe and, in displacing the middlebrow journals that had defined the pubic sphere since the 1850s, misconstrued the relationship of criticism and the public sphere; however, that critique began in the 1880s, when Howells and the influential Atlanta group faulted the "feminine"

Victorian sentimentality of Dickens, Hart, or Harriet Beecher Stowe and promoted the manly American realism of Twain and others. Steve Mailloux grants, by contrast, that the "cultural conversation" about the novel has changed markedly since the 1870s, when Twain and George W. Cable campaigned against black disenfranchisement. Mailloux assumes, however, that, despite these changes, the reader follows modernist practices, seeing through stock phrases and ideological discourses and grasping Twain's ironic or satirical ends. I have suggested, however, that since the 1870s the conditions governing interpretative practice have also changed. While the influential magazines in Atlanta group promoted the "manly" American realism of Twain and others, the universities defended a classical canon of literary works, African Americans suffered widespread disenfranchisement, women and minorities were deprived of basic rights, and industrial capitalism was forming monopolies that dominated the national economy. By the twentieth-first century, "private" literary criticism has displaced middlebrow magazines as arbiters of literary value; American public and higher education has been integrated; black, women's, and ethnic studies programs and literary traditions have been established; and the global economy has undermined the nation-state. In this context, multiple American canons provide competing definitions of what counts as American literature and even an American identity. Criticism can no longer simply add race, gender, or ethnicity to its analyses but must address what Henry Louis Gates, Jr., terms "the factitious nature of an 'American' identity." (103). In other words, instead of reconstructing the public sphere in a liberal manner or treating modernist practices as universal, the black studies that examine Twain's acceptance of the minstrel tradition or Jim's complex responses to Southern racism in light of these new American literatures effectively reevaluate the racial import of the novel. Perhaps that is why the eminent Twain scholar

Louis Budd considers such cultural diversity "a surgical strike . . . deadly to Twain, who interacted with his audiences much more intimately, in fact more physically than the high-culture authors in his time or today" (204). Budd assumes that Twain's public status overcomes all such divisions, but they bring out the limits of his otherwise great novel.

CHAPTER 5

RICHARD WRIGHT'S *NATIVE SON*

BETWEEN NATURALIST PROTEST AND MODERNIST LIBERATION

THE REVALUATION OF *HUCKLEBERRY FINN* DISCUSSED IN Chapter 4 shows that by the twentieth-first century, the global economy has undermined the nationalist ideals of the state, American public and higher education has been integrated, and black, women's, and ethnic studies programs and literary traditions provide competing definitions of what counts as American literature and an American. Scholars like Louis Budd assume that the public status of the great artist overcomes this multicultural diversity, but in this new context the multiple American canons justify the revaluation. Scholars also assume that the public character of *Native Son* overcomes this diversity, but in this case also the contrary readings that the novel acquires show the progressive influence of black studies and the black aesthetics movement.

What contradictory readings does the novel acquire? On the one hand, it is generally considered a naturalist protest novel in which Wright shows how racial discrimination and class oppression destroy Bigger Thomas, the novel's hero. On the other, it depicts Bigger's existential struggle for liberation.

As the contrary responses of many critics testify, these views are incompatible.[1] To treat the novel as protest fiction is to deny that Bigger wins liberation, whereas to treat the novel as a modernist or existential depiction of Bigger's liberation is to deny that the novel protests his oppression and victimization. In other words, if he is liberated, the system does not defeat him, whereas if the system defeats him, he does not liberate himself. A liberated victim is a contradiction in terms. Edward Margolies comments that "Wright does not seem to be able to make up his mind." He is "intellectually committed to" the communist views of Max the lawyer but "is more emotionally akin to Bigger's" existential views (79–80).[2]

Where does this indecision or opposition come from? What does it show? Scholars attribute it to Wright's changing beliefs. I will maintain, however, that what matters more than his beliefs are the changing status of the naturalist and modernist literary movements and the emergence of black aesthetics and black studies programs. In the 1930s, when Wright wrote *Uncle Tom's Children* and *Native Son*, the naturalist literary movement of Stephen Crane, Emile Zola, and Theodore Dreiser was very important and influential, whereas modernist fiction was considered experimental or regressive. It is not surprising, then, that, as many reviewers and critics pointed out, *Native Son* parallels Dreiser's *An American Tragedy*, which reveals the overwhelming social forces making a tragic victim of Clyde Griffith, its protagonist.[3] Like Clyde, Bigger Thomas, the protagonist of *Native Son*, falls victim to implacable social forces. It is, nonetheless, true that, because Wright's beliefs evolve, the status of naturalism and modernism changes, and black studies programs grow important, *Native Son* also parallels the modernist *Their Eyes Were Watching God* in that Janie Starks and Bigger achieve liberation.

PARALLELS OF *NATIVE SON* AND
AN AMERICAN TRAGEDY

Although *Native Son* and *An American Tragedy* both adopt the naturalist assumption that, in Donald Pizer's terms, "life place[s] tragic limitations on individual freedom, growth, and happiness" (29), the two novels differ in some important ways. Wright compresses his story, which begins on the morning when Bigger kills the rat terrifying his family and ends several months later when, sentenced to death on the electric chair, he bids his lawyer Max goodbye, whereas Dreiser elaborates his story, which starts when, as a child, Clyde Griffiths, along with his evangelical family, sings religious hymns on street corners, and ends when, a grown-up, he dies on the electric chair. Wright sticks strictly to the viewpoint of Bigger, whose feelings he explains, whereas Dreiser engages in an omniscient narration, which tells us why the Griffith family neglects Clyde and why the district attorney decides to prosecute him.

Despite these different artistic strategies, Clyde and Bigger have similar experiences: they reject their impoverished, religious families; pursue the American dream of wealth and ease; and, because of class or racial divisions, suffer tragic deaths on the electric chair. In *An American Tragedy* the poor family of Clyde proselytizes on street corners, soliciting donations and worshippers. Breaking with them, Clyde works at a soda fountain and then at luxurious Kansas City and Chicago hotels, which teach him to esteem the attentions of pretty girls and to value good clothes and a life of wealth and ease. The beautiful but cold and fickle Hortense Briggs fascinates him so much that he neglects his pregnant, abandoned sister Esta in order to buy Hortense a fur coat and other expensive goods. After the speeding car carrying him and the other bellhops to work accidentally kills a girl, he flees Chicago but does not abandon the pursuit of beautiful women or the life of luxury and ease. On the contrary, in the Kansas City hotel where he next finds work, he imagines a rich patron who "might take a fancy to him and offer him a connection with something important somewhere . . . and that might lift him into a world such as he had never known before" (188).

Bigger also rejects his poor religious family and seeks a wealthy patron who "might lift him into a world such as he had never known before." While his mother works and prays and his sister Vera attends sewing school, Bigger and his pals rob stores and in a game play important roles, such as U.S. president or an army general. In a scene that *Reader's Digest* edited out, a film about the promiscuous Mary Dalton and her communist lover Jan convinces him that, if he went to work for the wealthy Daltons, they would enable him to make his fortune. In other words, like Clyde, he seeks a life of great wealth, but, acting humble, he works as the Daltons' chauffeur, as his mother and "the relief" require him to.

Similarly, Clyde's mother advises him to write to his wealthy uncle Samuel Griffiths, who, when they meet at the Kansas City hotel, invites Clyde to work in his collar factory. In Lycurgus, the upstate New York hometown of the Griffiths, Clyde, esteemed by the factory workers but neglected by the Griffiths, dates Roberta Alden, a poor working woman whom he refuses to marry when he gets her pregnant, just as he declined to assist his pregnant sister Esta; at the same time, he pursues and wins the rich and beautiful Sandra Finchley, who, unlike the poor Roberta, can fulfill his dream of a marriage and provide him wealth and ease.

Similarly, Bigger has a relationship with the poor, working woman Bessie Mears, whom he also gets pregnant, and with the rich Mary Dalton, for whom he works as a chauffeur; however, while Clyde attracts Roberta and Sandra because of his rich relatives, Bigger interests Mary because of her communist sympathies. Clyde's submissive personality and intense adoration appeal to Sandra, whereas Mary and her communist lover Jan befriend Bigger out of a desire to understand and aid black people.

After Bigger and Clyde reject their religious families and get involved with worldly friends, they both find patrons or lovers who for very different reasons may realize their dreams of wealth and ease. Moreover, they both accidentally murder their lovers. Since Mary makes Bigger painfully aware of his race and since he believes that she really despises him, Bigger hates her but does not mean to kill her. In the unedited version, he carries the drunk and sexually aroused Mary to her room, where, aroused himself, he fondles her. Terrified when her blind mother comes in, he suffocates her as he tries to silence her with a pillow. Clyde too kills Roberta by accident, but initially he plans to kill her because he fears that, if she reveals her pregnancy, he would lose any chance of marrying Sandra and living the wealthy life. His feelings about her are, however, so ambivalent that he is unable to carry out his plan; instead, he lets her drown when, after he accidentally strikes her with his camera, she falls into the lake.

In these somewhat different ways, Clyde and Bigger both commit murder, and they both undergo trials in which the prosecuting attorneys stereotype them in order to gain political advantage, newspapers depict them as brutal killers, hostile mobs call for their lynching, and their mothers and religious figures try to save them. In both novels, the real issue is, then, not so much their death sentences as the oppression and class division victimizing Clyde and Bigger. The rural stereotypes and political strategizing, the false account of Roberta's death, the protection of the wealthy Griffiths, and the implacable mechanism of Clyde's prison underline the divisions of rich and poor destroying Clyde. Similarly the centuries of American racial and class oppression described by Max make Bigger a murderer and, hence, a victim.

As these parallels suggest, *Native Son* affirms the naturalist view that rigid class divisions cause individual tragedy, yet the novel also breaks with its naturalism. Although Clyde and Bigger are both moved by their trials and the intense national spotlight to examine themselves, their examinations go in contrary directions. Sentenced to death, abandoned by Sondra and his friends, and confined to a death-row cell block, Clyde plunges into despair. The prayers and admonitions of his mother, a strong religious woman, and Duncan McMillan, a young, energetic evangelist, support and restore him, moving him to reaffirm his rejected religious beliefs.

Bigger also examines his life, but, unlike Clyde, he repudiates religious salvation because it makes humanity guilty for its fallen state. Convinced by his mother and McMillan to turn to God to overcome his despair and terror, Clyde writes a farewell letter urging others to accept God. By contrast, Bigger resents the pastor sent by his mother and throws away the cross that the pastor has given him. As the narrator says, the "preacher's words . . . made him feel a sense of guilt deeper than that which even his murder of Mary had made him feel" (264).

Although Bigger rejects religion because of this unacceptable guilt, he accepts the humanist belief that human nature transcends the limits imposed by racial stereotypes. Initially he takes the stereotypes for granted; as the narrator says, "To Bigger and his kind, white people were not really people. They were a sort of great natural force like a stormy sky looming overhead" (109). Before the trial ends, he experiences an epiphany showing him the humanist truth: in a vision, he sees himself "standing in the midst of a vast crowd of men, white men and black men and all men, and the sun's rays melted away the many differences, the colors, the clothes, and drew what was common and good upward" (335). In other words, humanism becomes his new religion; as the narrator puts it, "The word had become flesh" (268).

In addition to this new humanism, he experiences a new, existential sense of liberation. For example, when he kills Mary and his girlfriend Bessie, he feels transformed: "He had murdered and created a new life for himself" (101). As critics point out, he embraces the murders as a way to free himself from cultural stereotypes or racial degradation (see Baker, "Introduction" 18; Fishburn 99; and Jackson 132–33). Since this new freedom opposes Max's communist view of liberation, Max faults him: "Bigger, you killed. That was wrong. It's too late now for you to . . . work with . . . others who are t-trying to . . . believe and make the world live again" (390). Shocking Max, Bigger rejects organized political activity and defends his newfound freedom: "What I killed for must have been good" (392).

The parallels of *The American Tragedy* and *Native Son* break down because, as the conflict of Max and Bigger suggests, the existential humanism of Bigger does not square with the novel's scientific naturalism.[4] The scientific naturalism that Wright shares with Dreiser makes Bigger a victim of large social forces, whereas the existential humanism freeing Bigger gives the novel what Craig Werner calls a "modernist subtext" in which the imagination defeats oppressive social circumstances (126; see also Costello 39–40; and Howe 139).

PARALLELS OF *NATIVE SON* AND *THEIR EYES WERE WATCHING GOD*

Since Wright reread Dostoevssky's novels while he was writing *Native Son*, some critics identify this subtext with Dostoevsky's *Crime and Punishment*, in which Raskolnikov also considers himself free to kill.[5] The subtext suggests, however, that, in addition, *Native Son* parallels Zora Neale Hurston's *Their Eyes Were Watching God*, which was published in 1936, four years before *Native Son*, and which also depicts sex, murder, and existential liberation.[6] Of course, *Their Eyes* is a problematic text. Wright condemned it for entertaining whites, instead of protesting racial or class oppression—Hurston famously rejected what she termed "the sobbing school of Negrohood who hold that nature somehow has given them a lowdown dirty deal" ("How It Feels" 153).

Moreover, *Their Eyes* approximates a romance such as *Pride and Prejudice*, rather than a naturalist protest novel. Both *Their Eyes* and *Pride* depict oppressive marriages and expose their causes—romantic illusions and misunderstandings. Both describe the female characters' difficulties, including the public and private selves into which they gradually divide and the public speech by which they overcome the division. For example, Elizabeth often engages in witty public discourse, freely disputing the opinions of one and all and thereby winning the ardent admiration of the wealthy Darcy, but, when she discovers that she has mistaken his character, she divides into a derisive public and an amorous private self.

Her marriage to Darcy overcomes this division and reinstates Enlightenment ideals. Because of her domineering husband Jodi Starks, Janie also divides into a public and private self, but she must struggle for the right to speak in public. Her struggle culminates when, after Joe calls her an old woman, she ridicules his sexual potency: "When you pull down yo' britches, you look lak du change uh life" (75). In shock, Jodi retreats to his bed, where he dies from a bad liver and a wounded ego. His death implies that, far from preserving Enlightenment ideals and middle-class propriety, Hurston's realism undermines them.

Instead of engaging in public speech, as Janie and Elizabeth do, Bigger fights with his pals or acts as a humble chauffer; however, he also divides into a public and private self and rejects Enlightenment ideals because he believes that killing

Mary Dalton frees him from his family's and his community's blindness. Moreover, Wright's third-person narration, which preserves the traditional distinction between standard English and the black dialect, implicitly justifies Bigger's view of the "blind" community. By contrast, in keeping with the Harlem Renaissance, which sought to demonstrate that black folk culture was not simply the subject of comic minstrelsy but worthy of serious artistic depiction, *Their Eyes* rejects the opposition of dialect and standard speech in the modernist fashion and depicts black speech and folk culture remarkably positively.

Although Bigger and Janie, despite their divided selves, achieve liberation, Bigger discovers that black culture is defeated and blind, whereas Janie learns to appreciate the rich values of ordinary black folk. This positive view of black folk emerges from Janie's intense, romantic relationship with Tea Cake. Initially he, like Jodi, treats her as a private possession, but, after she angrily protests such treatment, he teaches her the rich games, work, talk, music, and food of black folk culture. On the Florida muck, she learns to shoot a gun, pick beans, talk porch talk, and, in general, enjoy life. Although Tea Cake beats Janie and, along with Stew Beef, Sop-de-Bottom, and other friends, destroys the restaurant of the prejudiced Mrs. Turner, Janie finds the intense playing, fighting, working, socializing, and lovemaking fulfilling.

This naturalist utopia brings the "soul" of the fulfilled Janie "out of its hiding place" (122) but turns tragic when during a hurricane an overconfident Tea Cake braves the raging river only to be bitten by a mad dog and driven mad with rabies. Overcome with jealousy and thirst, he tries to shoot her, but she shoots him—a tragedy of immense proportions: "It was the meanest moment of eternity" (175).

While Wright's naturalism initiates what Michele Wallace terms a tradition of macho violence (55), this tragic moment implicitly faults Tea Cake's chauvinist violence and pride.

The tragedy suggests, in other words, that, despite the overwhelming circumstances, which the naturalist takes to defeat human aspirations, Janie achieves liberation. After her trial and Tea Cake's angry friends absolve her, she tells Phoeby the lessons of her independence: people must "go to God" and "find out about livin' fuh theyselves" (183). To save himself, Bigger also kills his girlfriend Bessie and affirms his independence, but at his unjust trial he is depicted as an animal and, despite Max's defense, is condemned to death. In that way *Native Son* both preserves the tragic character of circumstances and grants Bigger his liberation, which enables him, before he dies, to claim his killings must have been right and to send Jan his greetings, calling him Jan, not sir.

THE CHANGING CONTEXTS OF *NATIVE SON*

Native Son parallels Dreiser's *An American Tragedy*, which takes the class divisions of the rich and the poor to frustrate the aspirations of Clyde and to cause his tragic deaths, and Hurston's *Their Eyes*, which assumes that Janie overcomes the biases and conflicts of social life and achieves liberation. In other words, even though naturalism and modernism are incompatible, *Native Son* adopts both. What explains these contrary naturalist and modernist dimensions? The explanation lies, I will suggest, in the evolving beliefs of Wright, the changing status of naturalism and modernism, as well as the emergence of black studies programs.

In terms of Wright's beliefs, Max's views express the political commitment of Wright, who, in the 1930s, led the left-wing John Reed club and wrote articles for *The Worker* and other communist publications. Like many other radical African Americans, he favored the separate, Southern black nation advocated by the Communist Party and the autonomous national Soviet republics created by "Comrade Stalin" (Maxwell 6–8; see also Bell 152–54). By contrast, Wright's commitment to Bigger's liberation anticipates Wright's later work, in which he rejects communist politics and accepts individual existential and African national autonomy. As Margolies says, "It is . . . in the roles of a Negro nationalist revolutionary and a metaphysical rebel that Wright most successfully portrays Bigger" (82).

In other words, the opposition of naturalist social protest and modernist existential liberation echoes Wright's political evolution from a communist who believed that Marxism pointed a way "beyond race" to a black power advocate who defends black autonomy.[7] In addition, the opposition reflects the changes that the movements of modernism and naturalism and the types of literary criticism have undergone since the 1930s and 1940s.

At that time the naturalist movement was, as I noted, highly influential, whereas modernist works were labelled experimental or regressive and were held in low esteem. Influential left-wing critics faulted Hurston's *Their Eyes*, which, Wright said, "carries no theme, no message, no thought."[8] Hurston herself acquired the reputation of a simple, childlike, primitive "darkie" because she entertained and flattered her patron, Mrs. R. Osgood-Mason, a very controlling woman whom she called "godmother" (see Washington, Foreward 9–11). As a result, her work was forgotten. After World War II, Hurston, at the time the most prolific African American writer, worked as a maid and in 1959 died impoverished and forgotten. Her work was not recuperated until the 1970s, when Alice Walker, Toni Morrison, and black feminists repudiated protest fiction and revived her positive depictions of black life.

By contrast, *Native Son* made Wright famous and wealthy and influenced the next generation of black writers, including his critical friends Ralph Ellison and James Baldwin.

Initially Ellison claimed that, while Hurston's *Their Eyes* is marred by her "calculated burlesque," *Native Son* "possesses an artistry, penetration of thought, and sheer emotional power that places it in the front rank of American fiction" (in Gates and Appiah, *Wright* 15 and 12). Along with Baldwin, Ellison went on, however, to complain that the novel did not depict black humanity or intellectual and artistic independence in a positive way. In defense of the novel, Irving Howe and others argued that Wright's anger with blacks and whites truly reflected his debilitating experience of American social life and that in oedipal fashion Baldwin and Ellison were rebelling against their literary father.

Howe's view lost out, for Lionel Trilling, his fellow New York Intellectual, argued that naturalist protest fiction had gained high status because liberals mistakenly prefer "reality" to "mind," as their praise of Dreiser's work showed (23–24). Along with the New Critics, who established their dominance at that time and who also rejected naturalist fiction, Trilling complained that such "democratic" art does not provide "the sense of largeness, of cogency . . . of being reached in our secret and primitive minds" characterizing the work of Henry James and other modernists (*Liberal* 286). Morris Dickstein says that, because of these critiques, "seminal writers like Dreiser and Richard Wright were relegated to the shabby ghetto of propaganda, rather than art" (381).

In the 1960s and 1970s, newly established black studies programs rehabilitated *Native Son* but reversed the opposition of naturalist realism and existential modernism. As Alessandro Portelli says, "When the time came to rescue the novel for the burgeoning field of African American studies . . . Bigger was now most often described as a heroic self who achieves freedom and full humanity . . . rather than an inarticulate victim of his environment" (255). Houston Baker argues, for example, that the novel depicts Bigger as an existential hero and not as a naturalist victim. His development echoes the liberation depicted in nineteenth-century slave narratives. As Baker says, "Bigger's movement from bondage to freedom follows the same course: he repudiates white American culture, affirms black survival values, and serves as a model hero—a strong man getting stronger" (Introduction 5; see also Gayle 179). Moreover, Baker considers the novel's existentialism, rather than its naturalism, a realistic response to black life. As he says, "The fundamental conditions of black life in America led him to see that apriori moral values could scarcely be operating in the great scheme of events" (Introduction 18; see also Jackson 129; and JanMohammed 16–18).

While Baker also attributes Wright's communism to black life, especially the strong black community, Henry Louis Gates ridicules his Marxism, calling it a matter of "race and superstructure," and faults the novel's realism, which continues what Gates terms the black drive to justify the race's intelligence, instead of furthering the aesthetic devices of the black literary tradition (30). In this way Gates opposes the revaluation of *Native Son* but not the priority of modernist aesthetics over realist naturalism. More importantly, while Gates faults *Native Son*, he esteems *Their Eyes* because its figural devices and free indirect discourse initiate the multivoiced narration of black modernist art. Similarly, Robert Stepto praises Hurston's novel because it "forwards the historical consciousness of the tradition's narrative forms" (*Behind* 166).

While Baker justifies *Native Son*'s naturalist or Marxist realism on sociocultural grounds, Gates and Stepto esteem *Their Eyes* on modernist figural or rhetorical grounds; however, to revalue these novels, they assimilate them to black traditions and experience. Other critics revalue *Native Son* but dismiss its black contexts and the opposition of naturalism and modernism. Joyce Joyce claims, for instance, that Wright's artistic genius matters more than the novel's themes or politics. On this basis she construes the novel as a classical tragedy revealing the objective truths of human nature. As she says, a "blind seer," Bigger recognizes "the futility of looking outside the self for affirmation" and achieves thereby the dignity and tragic stature of an Oedipus (*Tragedy* 116). Moreover, she rejects both the "naturalist and existential views" of him: "Naturalistic and existential views of Bigger as either a victimized or isolated figure limit the dimensions of Bigger's character and give no attention to how Wright's use of language punctuates the irony and ambiguity of Bigger's personality" (*Tragedy* 172).[9]

Other critics also defend the novel's objective truth and fault black and naturalist/modernist notions of Bigger's "isolation" or liberation, but these critics emphasize the novel's historical insight into class and racial oppression, rather than its tragic character. For instance, unlike the many critics who fault Max's long, didactic speech, Barbara Foley defends it on realist grounds. It provides what *An American Tragedy* takes for granted: an objective critique of American racial and class oppression ("Politics" 195). Foley also dismisses Bigger's existential liberation, but more negative than Joyce, Foley terms it "a twisted assertion of identity which, in its very deviance, profoundly condemns the social circumstances which have . . . deprived Bigger of any coherent sense of self" ("Politics" 194; see also Burgum 122; and Decoste 133–43). While Joyce construes the novel as a modern tragedy, Foley takes it to reveal the racial and class oppression of the 1930s; nonetheless, unlike Gates, who situates the novel in the literary tradition justifying black intelligence, or Baker, who argues that Bigger's existential liberation as well as the novel's realist naturalism reflect black cultural practices, Foley and Joyce both dismiss the novel's modernism and naturalism on the grounds that the insights of the novel transcend literary genres and ethnic or racial differences and reveal the objective truths of human nature or capitalist society.

Along with Cornel West and others, Foley and Joyce argue, in addition, that Gates, Baker, and other black scholars accommodate the white literary establishment and neglect the community or the working class.[10] In West's terms, black studies repudiates "the African American literature of racial confrontation during the four decades of the forties to the seventies" because of "the existential needs and accommodating values of the black and white literary professional-managerial classes" (39).[11] Such critiques fail to consider, however, that, as the last chapter suggested, the modern university has acquired massive cultural influence undermining the common values or public sphere in terms of which Foley, Joyce, and others explain the novel's objective truth.

In the 1930s and 1940s, when middlebrow magazines like *Reader's Digest*, which published *Native Son*, still dominated the public sphere, Wright and other realists faulted fiction that, like the modernist *Their Eyes*, addressed "nationalist" cultural issues, and they justified naturalist protest fiction that, they maintained, would transform American social life. After World War II the New Critics, the New York Intellectuals, and other critics and scholars reversed these priorities, esteeming the work of conservative modernists and denigrating naturalist fiction. The New Critics, who dominated major American universities at that time, promoted the modernist avant-garde, but, as supporters of the Southern Agrarian movement, they defended the organic community and patriarchal traditions of the Old South and condemned the "progress," industry, liberalism, science, wealth, bureaucracy, and democratic equality of the Yankee North (see Jancovich 71–101). Allied with the New Critics, the New York intellectuals treated conservative modern writers as an oppositional force undermining the "indiscriminate" liberal faith in human equality and social justice. In the 1930s and 1940s, when liberals and communists struggled for racial equality and social progress, the New York Intellectuals, who included Sidney Hook, Lionel Trilling, Irving Howe, and James Burnham, defended Marxist and radical views. These scholars then reversed themselves, reducing communist practices to a nightmarish totalitarian other and liberal writers and critics to fellow travelers whose tolerance of communism showed their blindness to impending evil. Scholars point out that, fearing an oppressive cultural decline, a broad range of critics also justified the subversive force of modern high art and dismissed naturalist protest fiction and popular culture (see Huyssen 26; Norris 242; Pietz 65; Ross 42–64; Schaub 17; and Sinfield 102).

It was not until the 1960s and 1970s that, thanks to the black power and civil rights movements, student rebellions, rapidly expanding American universities, and an unusually prosperous economy, African American literary study established itself in academia and revalued *Native Son*. At that time, it underwent what Baker terms a "paradigm shift": the black power movement gave rise to a new black aesthetics, which dismissed the realist belief that African American literature adhered to common American ideals and that identified African American literature with peculiarly African American experience, culture, language, and history (*Blues* 76–7). This paradigm shift came too late for Hurston, whose work was, as I noted, reclaimed by Alice Walker and other black feminists, not by the black aestheticists; nonetheless, this shift, which "made it possible for literary-critical and literary-theoretical investigators to . . . include previously 'unfamiliar' objects in an expanded (and sharply modified) American art world," justified the reinterpretation of *Their Eyes* and *Native Son* as novels of liberation.[12]

The New York Intellectuals, who adopted modernist accounts of American or Western culture, dismissed not only naturalist protest and popular "mass" fiction but also this "nationalist" African American studies as well as women's, ethnic, and postcolonial studies and poststructuralist theories. By the 1980s and 1990s, when conservative politicians increasingly dominated federal and state government and the global economy was absorbing American industry and finance, scholars went on to blame the universities' expanding disciplines, black, women's, or ethnic studies, or multicultural clientele for the humanities' growing fragmentation and declining public support. I discussed the issues raised by these "culture wars" in the introduction;[13] suffice it to say that, although corporate elites dominate the increasingly privatized university of the twenty-first century, the cultural influence that the modern university has acquired since World War II has given literary scholars the ability to influence their professional and nonprofessional communities in positive ways. In other words, instead of co-opting black scholars or rendering them irrational, the modern university has given them new import or importance. Along with Wright's changing beliefs and modernism's and naturalism's new status, this new import explains why *Native Son*'s naturalist version, in which racial and class oppression victimize Bigger, is incompatible with its modernist version, in which Bigger overcomes his oppression and liberates himself.

The accounts of Joyce, Foley, and others mean to preserve the traditional public sphere, but, to establish the novel's universal or historical truth, they dismiss the "debilitating" influence of literary movements, black studies, and the university. By contrast, the accounts of Baker and others suggest that African American experience justifies the novel's existential view of Bigger's liberation as well as the contrary naturalist account of his tragic racial and class oppression. In other words, the accounts of *Native Son* based on black studies have revalued the naturalist and the existential versions of the novel and, as a result, these accounts effectively foster the excluded cultures and oppositional movements of the black community.[14] The next chapter will show that the emergence of black feminism legitimates a similar revaluation of Faulkner's and Morrison's work.

CHAPTER 6

IDENTITY AND CONVENTION IN FAULKNER'S *LIGHT IN AUGUST* AND MORRISON'S *JAZZ*

PREVIOUS CHAPTERS SUGGESTED THAT THE NATURAL SCIENCES' domination of the modern university motivated the revaluation of *Frankenstein* and the emergence and influence of black studies explain the contrary versions of *Native Son*. In a similar way, this chapter suggests that the evolution of black feminism explains the revaluation and reinterpretation of William Faulkner's and Toni Morrison's fiction. In the 1940s, when the New Critics first established the canonical status of William Faulkner's work, they appreciated his pessimism, which reveals what John Crowe Ransom called the "moral confusion" of the "modern world"—it can "look back nostalgically upon the old world of traditional values and feel loss and perhaps despair" (112). In the 1990s, when the success of Toni Morrison had generated important new studies of her work and Faulkner's, scholars suggested that, as Carol A. Kolmerton says, "Read together, the fiction of Faulkner and Morrison offers a richly varied and profoundly moving meditation on racial, cultural, and gender issues in twentieth-century America." While the New Critics claimed that his works "look back nostalgically" upon the Old South's "world of traditional values," modern critics take the contrary view: taken together, his work and Morrison's offer a "richly varied and profoundly moving meditation on racial, cultural, and gender issues."

Some of these modern critics go on, however, to treat Faulkner and Morrison as equally profound and creative geniuses who rise above their cultural contexts and grasp the common truths of our human nature or racial and sexual contexts.[1] As Philip Weinstein says, Faulkner and Morrison transcend their "distinctive racial and gender positioning" and, far from failing "their potential, . . . achieve it, becoming Faulkner and Morrison" (162). Other critics maintain that gothic romances and hardboiled mysteries provide the intertextual conventions illustrating and justifying their (re) interpretation as "a richly varied and profoundly moving meditation on racial, cultural, and gender issues in twentieth-century America."[2] Far from showing that Faulkner and Morrison transcend their "distinctive racial and gender positioning," this reinterpretation indicates that American reading practices evolved from the New Criticism, which first established Faulkner's reputation in the 1940s, to black feminism, which recognized Morrison's value in the 1980s.

FAULKNER'S *LIGHT IN AUGUST* AND MORRISON'S *JAZZ*

The revaluation of Faulkner's *Light in August* and Morrison's *Jazz*, in particular, is based on the novels' shared conventions. Like detective fiction, *Light in August* and *Jazz* describe crimes and criminals in a realistic fashion but, instead of investigating at length who the culprit is or treating the culprit as demonic and the law as just, these novels problematize the identity of the culprits, who are outsiders or marginal figures unable to accept traditional middle-class or liberal values. Although *Native Son* also depicts the problematic history and identity that make Bigger Thomas a sympathetic murderer, as naturalist fiction, the naturalist *Native Son* protests the oppressive circumstances making the protagonist a victim. By contrast, the Faulkner and Morrison novels preserve an imaginative optimism whereby characters break with traditional racial and sexual categories to affirm themselves or to improve their lives. More precisely, because of its modernist pessimism *Light in August* ambiguously affirms human will and imagination, whereas *Jazz* expresses a decidedly optimistic view of them.

Like other Faulkner and Morrison novels, *Absalom, Absalom!* and *Beloved* also rework their generic conventions, which in their case include the multiple narrators, tormented lovers, dominating figures, spiritual exorcisms, and haunted houses of the gothic romance. To very different extents, these novels also preserve an imaginative optimism whereby characters break with traditional racial and sexual categories to affirm themselves or to improve their lives. The postmodern *Jazz* goes on, however, to dissolve the distinctions between the individual and the community, the narrator and the characters, and the city and the country.

As I will show, traditional critics emphasize the novels' formal autonomy, internal textual or figural import, unifying authorial intention, and historical insightand may deny or reject any postmodern import, which reduces, they argue, to an irrational identity politics. Other critics grant that these novels rework those and other literary conventions and, as a result, consider *Jazz* a forceful postmodern novel. I will suggest, however, that it is changing

American reading practices, not those figural devices or literary conventions, that explain the novels' revaluation and reinterpretation.

LOVE, JUSTICE, AND TRUTH IN
LIGHT IN AUGUST (1932)

Accounts of *Light in August* and *Jazz* evolve from the traditional to the postmodern view, including the dissolution of narrative conventions and affirmation of community. On the one hand, some "contemporary" critics maintain that in *Light in August*, for example, the outsiders resist the community and affirm themselves and that the novel critiques its literary discourses, including the conventions of detective and naturalist fiction. On the other, more traditional critics argue that in *Light in August* the community excludes the outsiders and preserves its integrity and well as the text's unity or integrity.

To summarize the traditional perspective, the novel contrasts the tragic stories of Joe Christmas and Gail Hightower with the comic narrative of the wandering Lena Grove. For example, in Christmas's story, which emerges from Mrs. Hines's account and from Christmas's memories, Doc Hines, a mad Calvinist fanatic who is his grandfather, kidnaps Joe and leaves him at a Memphis orphanage, where Hines, who works there as a janitor, calls Joe a "nigger" because his father was Mexican. Since the orphanage's dietician, who fears that the young Joe saw her having sex with a doctor, agrees with Hines, the orphanage arranges for him to be adopted by McEachern, a Calvinist farmer, who teaches him to despise religion, women, and sex.

Bobby the waitress and prostitute also teaches him about women and sex, but, after Joe kills McEachern at a dance and, exulting, rides his slow, white horse triumphantly into town, Bobby curses him, and her employers beat him because the killing has ruined their business. Providing another lesson, his love affair with Joanna Burden repeats his earlier experiences with Bobby and McEachern. When he eats dinner in Burden's dark kitchen, he gets irritated and angrily throws the plates of food that she has provided him at the wall. Sex with a "negro" excites Burden so much that she leaves him secret letters and arranges for him to find her naked in various places. He fears, however, that she sucks him into a bottomless pit, a metaphoric version of the loss of self with which Mrs. McEachern threatened him. After her desire cools, she tries to shoot him and herself, but he cuts her throat because, like McEachern, she tries to pray over him. He successfully evades the sheriff and his hounds pursuing him, but, instead of fleeing, goes to Mottstown and surrenders to the sheriff. Before his trial he escapes, only to let the protofascist Grimm butcher him.

The story of Hightower, a former minister who refuses to leave Jefferson even after Klansmen beat him, is less dramatic but equally tragic. After his reputation has been ruined by his wife's infidelity and suicide and his obsession with his grandfather, a Confederate General, who, after the Civil War, was killed while stealing chickens, he is reduced to an outsider. Imagining the congregation entering the church, Hightower considers their religion a quest for death, but he too withdraws from life because he assumes that history stopped with his grandfather's death.

Contrasting with Joe Christmas's and Gail Hightower's tragic stories, the narrative of the wandering Lena Grove, who endlessly pursues her fleeing lover Lucas Burch (aka Joe Brown), is comic. The novel describes her as a woman of nature or earth because she trusts in the community's generosity instead of looking out for herself (23). She anticipates and readily accepts the assistance of Armisted, who gives her a ride and puts her up at his house, and of Armisted's wife Martha, who gives Lena her savings but won't have breakfast with her. Lena mixes up Byron Bunch and Burch/Brown, but, once Bunch inadvertently reveals that Brown is Burch—the white scar betrays him—Lena remains faithful to Brown even though he flees her. At the end, the furniture repairer, who depicts Lena and Byron continuing their pursuit of Burch/Brown, emphasizes the comedy of Lena's constancy. She does not want Bryon to leave her, but she refuses to marry him or to engage in sexual activity with him.

In short, the traditional approach suggests that the novel weaves together the comic narrative of Lena with the tragic narratives of Christmas and Hightower. The trouble is, however, that the accounts from which these coherent narratives are derived differ sharply. For example, as Lena Grove rides in Armisted's cart, she sees the smoke from Annie Burden's burning house. A symbol unifying her story and that of Joe Christmas, the smoke indicates that, as the novel eventually shows, the murder of Annie Burden has already taken place and that in a sense the novel is a detective story which will explain the crime;however, the narrators give us various explanations but provide no objective solution of the murder or the murderer.

From Joe Brown, Byron Bunch, the dietician, Mr. McEachern, and Joe Christmas to Joanne Burden and the furniture repairer, the various narrators give us diverse explanations, not a definitive account. The Calvinists McEachern and Doc Hines claim to know what God believes and demands, identify white males as the elect, and condemn women and blacks as "womanfilth," "whore," "lecherer," "nigger," "nigger lover," "devil," or "harlot." The Calvinists assume—in other words, believe—that they grasp the truth and the justice of God, yet we experience their views as just another perspective. The narrator tells us, for example, that, when Joe Christmas kills McEachern with a chair, he walks into nothingness: "Perhaps the nothingness astonished him a little, but not much, and not for long" (178).

The explanations of the other narrators, who include Christmas, Gail Hightower, Byron Bunch, Joanna Burden, and Lena Grove, accept the Freudian belief that the reactions of an adult repeat his or her experiences as a child. In Faulkner's terms, "memory believes before knowing remembers" (104). In that sense, the past dominates the present, so that a character's capacity to escape the past becomes a pressing issue.

Moreover, far from treating the culprit as an evil or depraved figure, as detective fiction usually does, the narrators of *Light in August*, who are all outsiders or marginal, if not criminal or immoral, figures, are able, to different degrees, to engage the reader's sympathies, especially if they succeed in escaping the past. For example, a passing farmer, who finds Burden's house burning and her head almost cut off, also finds Brown there, but not Joe, who has wandered off. The sheriff assumes, nonetheless, that Christmas killed her because Brown reveals that Christmas is "a nigger," not the white person that the community took him to be.

Despite the gruesome murder, such racial prejudice, along with Christmas's mistreatment by Hines, the dietician, McEachern, and others, makes him sympathetic. Moreover, his story concludes with an existential affirmation in which he finally breaks what he terms the circle of his life. After he surrenders to the sheriff and is put in jail, the townspeople complain that at Mottstown he did not act like a black or a white person. Hines calls him an abomination and urges the townspeople to hang him because a mixed-race person does not fit into Hines's absolute categories of white and black. Similarly, to explain why he let the protofascist

Grimm butcher him, Gavin Stevens the lawyer describes an unending battle between his black and his white blood (393). The narrator suggests, however, that at the end Joe breaks with the past and, like Camus's Mersault, achieves a kind of stoic resolution in that, when he surrenders to the Mottstown sheriff, he breaks the circle of his life. In *As I Lay Dying*, the Bundrens' equally disruptive trip to Jefferson costs Jewel his horse, Cash, his leg, Darl, his sanity, but brings Anse new teeth and a new wife. More forceful and positive, Christmas's escape from his life's circle costs him his life but brings him an unexpected immortality; as Faulkner says, "the man seemed to rise soaring into their memories forever and ever" (407).

Hightower, by contrast, remains unable to escape the past, but he too affirms himself when he gets involved with Lena and Christmas. He urges Byron not to marry Lena, whom he considers a fallen woman, but, when she gives birth, he acts as her midwife. When Mrs. Hines asks him to say that Christmas was with him the night of Joanna's murder, he refuses to lie, yet, to stop Grimm from killing Christmas, he says that that night Christmas was with him.

In these and other ways, the novel grants Christmas, Hightower, and others a stoic affirmation that undermines the evil villains and definitive solutions of detective fiction. Traditional critics claim, however, that, far from granting the outsiders such affirmations, the community excludes them and preserves its and, hence, the novel's unity. In "The Community and the Pariah," Cleanth Brooks maintains, for example, that the violent outsiders are defeated. He considers the novel "a bloody violent pastoral" in which the traditional Southern community preserves its common sense and excludes the "outcasts, pariahs, defiant exiles, withdrawn quietists, or strangers" whose isolation explains their perversion or sterility (55, 65–66). As he says, "The plight of the lost sheep and of the black sheep can be given special point and meaning because there is still visible in the background a recognizable flock with its shepherds, its watchdogs, sometimes fierce and cruel, and its bellwethers" (56; see also Berland 4 and Warren 112–13). André Bleikasten complains that this notion of the "flock with its shepherds, its watchdogs, sometimes fierce and cruel, and its bellwethers" idealizes the community, whose commonsense includes not only complicity and conformity with puritan fanaticism and brutal racist and sexist violence but also unjust exclusion and condemnation of "the wretched of the earth" (82). Bleikasten faults Brooks's idealization of the community, but he too preserves its unity and autonomy and, hence, that of the novel. In place of the "recognizable flock with its shepherds, its watchdogs, . . . and its bellwethers," he substitutes the "closed society" whose racist and sexist ideology and fanatical puritanism dominates the community, enforcing its norms and excluding ambiguous figures like Joe Christmas and Joanna Burden (see also Berland 33).

In a feminist manner Patricia McKee examines the novel's racial or sexual discourse, but she too assumes that the society defeats its rebels. Explaining the gaze constructed by the media, she says that only white men do the looking that has public import, and that, read and exchanged, their looks are the means of their knowledge. McKee also grants that society destroys the men, as Brooks and Bleikasten argue, but she claims that their destruction results from their acting as martyrs to a lost cause.

Michael Millgate allows, by contrast, that Christmas achieves a stoic resolution that contradicts the community's racial categories and that Joanna Burden reveals a complexity that undermines the community's "rigid categorization" (43). Millgate claims, moreover, that, loaded with "characters and sequences," including the detective novel, the pastoral, and other generic types as well, *Light in August* is not a unified whole; rather, it leaves many puzzles unresolved and provides many conflicting viewpoints, instead of a definitive solution. In the traditional fashion, Millgate still argues, however, that Faulkner meant Lena's seduction and travels to acquire a timeless permanence (35), her biological compulsion to be "universally valid" (36), and the novel's mythic associations (40) and Hightower's moral reflections (39) to universalize the novel's theme.

Judith Wittenberg also grants that the characters resist the community's values, but she argues that "Faulkner not only provides a provocative consideration of the issues surrounding racial notions in the American South . . . indeed, in Western culture generally . . . he also manages to explore the role of language in the construction of subjectivity" (146–47). She shows that, based on "the Father-God, the Church, the adoptive father, the biological father, or the would-be surrogate father," what she terms "male ideas and language" dominate the characters' minds, producing violently repressive and destructive results. While the text undermines this language, exposing its inadequacy, the text also shows, she says, that the language destroys the characters who resist it. More negative than Bleikasten, she concludes that "flight, death, or perpetual apartness are the outcome of such assaults on the system" (163).

While Wittenberg claims that the novel undermines its cultural discourse, Millgate shows that it reworks the conventions of detective fiction and other genres; they both say, however, that the main characters resist social norms and affirm themselves. Despite very different views of the community, Brooks, Bleikasten, and McKee maintain, by contrast, that its norms defeat the rebellious characters and preserve its unity and the text's.

MURDER, LOVE, AND RACE IN *JAZZ*

Traditional and contemporary accounts of *Jazz* reveal similar differences. Joe and Violet Trace, its main characters, are also violent but sympathetic outsiders whose history and motivations undermine the conventional assumption that the criminal is demonic and that the crime has a scientific solution. In *The Bluest Eye*, Morrison's first novel, Cholly Breedlove too is a violent but sympathetic outsider. He was abandoned by his mother, rejected by his father, and tormented when first making love, but he fights with Mrs. Breedlove, rapes his daughter Pecola, and dies in the workhouse. Moreover, after Cholly rapes her, the community excludes her, and, despite her blue eyes, she degenerates into insanity. By contrast, more optimistic than this novel or *Light in August*, which grants Christmas, Hightower, and others only a stoic affirmation, *Jazz* shows that Violet and Joe successfully overcome the parental failures and racial prejudices of their past and reestablish a warm marital relationship.

While some accounts emphasize this "postmodern" subversion and affirmation, other, more traditional accounts situate the novel in its African American contexts and emphasize its textual unity or historical objectivity. To summarize the traditional account, the narrator explains that the relationship of Joe and Violet began when, after falling out of a tree near her, he spent most of the night joking with Violet, who then claimed him as her man. They moved north to the city because there, the narrator tells us, blacks make good money and own whole streets and Booker T. Washington has dined in the White House. During a riot there, a white man saves Joe from a pipe about to strike his head, yet Joe speaks of inventing himself anew in the city. With his young lover Dorcas he believes that he does that.

While Joe tries to reinvent himself in the city, Violet, who talks to her birds and grow silent and uncommunicative, blames the city for her faults. She says she messed up her life because she thought she was still young and ought not to have children, ensuring thereby that the world would not have fewer orphans. To explain her pessimism, the narrator says that Violet's mother Rose Dear lost her house when her husband ran off. Her grandmother True Belle came down from Chicago to help maintain the household, but Rose Dear committed suicide four years later. The narrator grants that Violet gradually loses her anger or outrage and grows silent but says that at times she has her "cracks" or acts crazy when, for example, she regrets her decision not to have children and almost steals a baby because she hopes that Joe would love it and her along with it (19–22).

By contrast, Dorcas's aunt Alice, trains Dorcas, who lost her parents during a riot, to resist the city's evils, but the narrator says that Alice was "no match for the city," which said "Come and do wrong" (67). Like Sula, who watched her mother burn, Dorcas, who watched her dolls burn up and not get a funeral, finds sin interesting. She accepts Joe as her lover but eventually tells him that she prefers a boy named Acton because the other girls envy her relationship with him and because she could not tell them about Joe. When she disappears, he tracks her to the crowded dance hall where he shoots her while she is happily dancing with the esteemed Acton.

Joe, who, after shooting Dorcas, spends days by his apartment window crying about his loss, explains that he did not know how to love; however, the narrator blames the light-skin prejudice of Joe's family and his painful rejection by his mother Wilde, a character whom Morrison initially meant to account for Beloved's fate after she flees 124 Bluestone.

As the narrator explains, the prejudice develops when the father of the white, wealthy Miss Vera Louise disowned her because she had a black lover, Henry Lestory or Le Story, and a mixed-race child, Golden Gray. Along with True Belle, the grandmother who ran the household of Violet after her father left and her mother lost the house, she moved to Baltimore, where she raised and idolized Golden Gray. Shocked to learn that his father is black, Grey traveled to his father's house to confront him. Just as Grey got there, a naked black woman, trying to escape him, ran into a tree and knocked herself out. When Henry returned home and met his son Grey for the first time, Wild gave birth to Joe, who was called Trace because his mother vanished without a trace. Unlike Joe Christmas, whose alleged miscegenation denies him a place in his family or the community, the mixed-race Henry Lestory or Hunter's Hunter, who is both a family friend and Joe's virtual father, accepts Joe, teaching him to hunt in and to love the woods and hinting that Wild is his mother. Before Joe and Violet leave for the city, Joe looks for Wild several times, but she won't reveal herself even though he begs her to.

This painful rejection explains why Joe shot Dorcas after she rejected him and why he mourns her loss. Moreover, as Violet suggests, this family history explains why Joe prefers the light-skinned Dorcas to her dark self and, since True Belle has told her so much about Golden Grey, why she shares this prejudice (97).

In the traditional account this history of the black family's prejudice explains the relationship of Joe and Violet and the murder of Dorcas; the involved narrator describes, however, not only the history and motivation of Joe, Violet, Alice, and Dorcas, but also the nature of "the City." Like Watson, Marlowe, and other involved narrators of a detective story, he praises the city, which, he says, gives blacks jobs and contains "amiable strangers." He fears, just the same, that, instead of establishing the truth, he has been misunderstood or misled by the characters. For instance, surprising the narrator, Felice explains the faults of her friend Dorcas and frees Joe and Violet as well as herself to improve themselves. She reveals not only that Dorcas thought only about how she won Acton or how she could get money for Acton and buy him things, but also that she let herself die because, when she was shot, she would not reveal Joe's name or let Felice call an ambulance. Thanks to this explanation, Joe revives, working at night and during the day roaming the city with Violet. While the narrator, who expected their relationship to remain sour, complains that he did not really understand the characters, Joe and Violet reestablish their relationship.

Some accounts of *Jazz* emphasize this postmodern subversion and affirmation, while other, more traditional accounts situate the novel in its African American contexts and do not acknowledge the subversion.[3] For example, emphasizing the novel's African American context, Angela Burton argues that, to reformulate the "mixed-race figure" the novel depicts the "abjection" whereby miscegenation breaks down the boundaries of self and other (173). Burton points out that the novel describes Dorcas as "sugar flawed" not to denote her light skin color but to indicate that her parents were raped by white slaveholders (177). The Creole influence on jazz music and the mixed-race groupings in 1920s Harlem night clubs also highlight, Burton says, the miscegenation behind mixed-race figures (177–78). Similarly, Golden Grey's oedipal desire to kill his black father Lestory breaks down his white sense of himself because he can recognizes his father as human only by reversing "white ideology"(181–83). The African American context becomes all the more important because Burton takes the relationship of Golden Grey and

Lestory not only to explain the novel's "narratives of identity" but also to free readers from their complicity with white power and white ideology (187–88).

While Burton considers Creole jazz and 1920s Harlem nightclubs the origins of the novel's aesthetics and the Golden Grey–Lestory relationship the foundation of the novel, endowing it with transformative force, Roberta Rubenstein says that it improvises on the modernist techniques of Faulkner and others. Charles Bon and Golden Grey are both effeminate, mixed-race characters who seek legitimation by their fathers, but, unlike Sutpen, the black Lestory repudiates his white son by demanding that he give up his white privileges. Moreover, just as Bon seeks recognition from his father, Joe Trace wants recognition from his mother Wild and from his young lover Dorcas, who, like his mother, deserted him.

Rubenstein says, moreover, that the novel involves multiple narratives as well as a postmodern aesthetic playfulness or artifice, not one single truth (151). The narrative paradoxically implies, she maintains, positions that are inside the story and, hence, modernist as well as outside of it and, hence, postmodernist (152). While the internal, modernist narratives draw the reader into the characters' psychology, the external, postmodern devices deny that we can know the stories of the characters. Moreover, since the narrator, an impersonal voice, grants that his speculations have no grounds in fact and complains that the characters misled and elude him (156, 161–62), the narrator gives the reader, Rubenstein says, the responsibility of constructing the novel's meaning.

In general, some critics emphasize the textual or figural import, the author's intentions, or the historical context of both *Light in August* and *Jazz*, while other critics claim, by contrast, that these novels rework the conventions of horror, detective, naturalist, or modernist fiction. The first account suggests that *Light in August* and *Jazz* describe crimes and criminals, but far from condemning or demonizing the killer, as many detective novels do, these novels sympathetically examine the background or history of the criminal as well as the victim and others in the community and, as a result, undermine traditional liberal values. The second account also says that in the two novels the violent outsiders do not amount to criminals or justify the conventional norms of justice; however, the second account suggests that, while *Light in August* preserves a modernist pessimism, *Jazz* emphasizes the limitations and misunderstandings of the narrator and the ability of the characters to overcome the past and improve their lives.

What explains this shift from a modernist pessimism to a postmodern affirmation? To summarize this evolution briefly, in the 1930s, when Faulkner wrote *Absalom!* and *Light in August*, the naturalist literary movement was, as I noted in the last chapter, very influential, whereas, held in low esteem, modernist works were considered experimental or regressive. At that time a number of critics complained, as a consequence, that in *Light in August* and other novels Faulkner indulges a "cult of cruelty" or ignores historical conflict or class differences (see Emerson 73–129). As the left-wing Granville Hicks said, the world of Faulkner "echoes with the hideous trampling march of lust and disease, brutality, and death" (cited in Schwartz, "Creating" 15).

Because of this negative criticism, in the early 1940s Faulkner's work went out of print, and Faulkner himself worked as a Hollywood screenwriter. By the 1950s the New Criticism, which became the hegemonic literary approach, revalued Faulkner's fiction—Cleanth Brooks considered Faulkner the greatest American novelist and *Light in August* the greatest American novel.

The New York Intellectuals faulted the security and careerist orientation of this specialized academic practice and defended the political responsibilities of the traditional public scholar; nonetheless, to secure positions in the university, the New York Intellectuals aligned themselves with the New Criticism, turning high modern art into what Lionel Trilling called "a polemical concept" (*Sincerity* 94). Howe, for example, provided what Lawrence Schwartz terms "the sharpest definition of Faulkner's role in the 'vital center' of politics and culture" (208).

Moreover, as I also noted in the last chapter, when black studies was established in 1960s and 1970s, African American literary criticism underwent what Houston Baker terms a "paradigm shift": a new black aesthetics dismissed the realist belief that African American literature adhered to common American ideals and identified African American literature with peculiarly African American experience, culture, language, and history.[4] Such a paradigm shift explains how Morrison's fiction came to be included in what Baker terms "an expanded (and sharply modified) American artworld"; still, black feminism, not the black aesthetic movement, established the high status of Morrison's work, which, in turn, legitimated the oppositional character of this black feminism. As Nancy Peterson points out, the evolution of black feminist criticism enabled Morrison's novels to receive in the 1980s the attention which they so terribly lacked in the 1970s (5). Ironically, Morrison contributed substantially to this evolution. As an editor at Random House, whose works influential magazines are very likely to review, she published the writings of Toni Cade Bambara, Angela Davis, and Gayle Jones, among others.[5] This work too has contributed markedly to the black feminist discourse producing her reputation. Moreover, like T. S. Eliot, whose revaluation of John Donne and the metaphysical poets sup-ported his modernist poetry, she has produced collections of nonfiction essays that, like *Race-ing Justice, En-gendering Power* and *Playing in the Dark: Whiteness and the Literary Imagination*, foster the black feminist concerns and issues justifying her work.

The work of Faulkner and Morrison was reinterpreted and revalued because of this black feminism, which treated her postmodern aesthetics as a positive form. In *The Shape of the Signifier* Michaels objects, however, that in her aesthetics the notion of "rememory" says that people can remember slavery, miscegenation, or other past events that their race or people have experienced but they themselves have not (135–39). Michaels complains that, as a result, her view of history imposes cultural identity and destroys the ideals of liberalism, which, until communism's collapse, forcefully emphasized ideological differences and economic inequality, rather than cultural differences. As he says, "Only at the end of history could all politics become identity politics" (24).[6]

Jazz suggests, however, that the characters remember the history of their family as well as their race. If identity politics has displaced the rational debate of the liberal tra-dition, it is not because of communism's breakdown. (As the famous question "Are you now or have you ever been a Communist?" suggests, far from a rational debate, it was blacklists, prison sentences, indoctrination, and warfare that usually resolved the ideological differences of communists and anticommunists.) Instead, the cultural influence that the modern university has acquired since World War II has destroyed the ability of literary scholars to address the public sphere in traditional ways. In other words, the contemporary or postmodern reading practices explaining *Jazz*'s account of the characters' family history and, more generally, of the black experience suggest that the increased influence of the modern university undermines the traditional distinctions between the objective and the subjective, the public and the private, or high and popular art. At the same time, this influence, not entirely bad, justifies the reading practices' reinterpretation and reevaluation of the novels. As these accounts suggested, although *Light in August* and *Jazz* both show that violent outsiders do not amount to criminals or support the conventional norms of justice, *Light in August* preserves a modernist pessimism, whereas, more optimistic, the postmodern *Jazz* emphasizes the characters' ability to overcome the past and improve their lives.

CHAPTER 7

THE POLITICS OF SARA PARETSKY'S DETECTIVE FICTION

IN CHAPTER 6, CHANGING READING PRACTICES, ESPECIALLY the emergence of black feminism, show that, contrary to traditional accounts, *Light in August* and *Jazz* both subvert the conventions of detective and naturalist fiction. In these novels violent outsiders do not amount to criminals or justify the conventional norms of justice. More fully than *Light in August*, which preserves the modernist pessimism of *Absalom, Absalom!*, *Jazz* emphasizes, at the same time, the characters' ability to overcome the past and improve their lives and undermines the distinctions between the individual and the community, the narrator and the characters, and the city and the country.

In an equally postmodern fashion, the mysteries of Sarah Paretsky subvert their generic conventions, but her works challenge the conventional belief that, unlike high art, which appeals to the few because it undermines its generic conventions or mainstream ideologies, popular culture ensures its popularity by conforming with established conventions and ideologies.

No one denies the popularity of her mysteries, which have spent many weeks on the best seller lists, been published in thirteen countries, and produced a worldwide network of fan clubs. What is at issue are the popularity's sources. Some reviewers credit Paretsky's feminism. As Michelle Green says, "Beneath that Dresden china exterior . . . is an ardent feminist with a magnum intellect and the guts to go where other doctorates fear to tread" (132; see also Koch 135). Preserving the conventional view, others say that her fiction is popular because it conforms with its generic conventions and, hence, its readers' traditional beliefs. LeRoy Panek claims, for example, that Paretsky uses "the conventions of detective and hard-boiled fiction" to show "the essential truths about character and the world contained in the best hard-boiled fiction" (84).[1] I will argue, by contrast, that what explains the popularity of her fiction is Paretsky's critique of the genre's conventions. Because the readers of fiction, who in the early twentieth century were mainly male high school graduates, now include a growing number of college-educated women, Paretsky's novels can challenge the conventions by which readers understand them and still achieve popularity. The self-doubt, restrained sexuality, persistent investigation, community of friends, and social criticism of V. I. Warshawski, Paretsky's female detective, subvert the traditional ideals whereby the detective hero who preserves his or her certainty, impersonality, self-control, sexual intensity, and an anarchic or uncommitted lifestyle accepts the liberal, middle-class faith in impartial justice and, thereby, restores justice to an unjust world.[2] While *Frankenstein*'s many popular movie and stage versions, along with the humanist opposition to science's domination, enabled the novel to challenge its generic conventions, the growing sophistication of Paretsky's readers and the increased influence of the modern university allow her fiction to subvert not only its generic conventions but also the conventional distinctions between the text and the reader, the academic and the ordinary, or the public and the private.

PARETSKY'S FICTION AND THE GENERIC CONVENTIONS OF MYSTERIES

For instance, Paretsky's novels undermine the characteristically anomic relationships of Mike Hammer or Philip Marlowe, who acquire reliable "buddies" but not close friends. In *Farewell, My Lovely*, for example, Marlowe confides in Red the boatman, sharing his desire for a moral crusade wiping out corruption, but, after Red helps him get into Brunette's gambling boat, Marlowe sees little of Red. V. I. maintains, by contrast, a supporting circle of intimate friends, who include Dr. Lotty Herschel, the reporter Murray Ryerson, and in later novels the neighbor Mr. Contreras and his golden retriever Peppy. When the muscle men hired by the criminals threaten, beat up, or seriously injure V. I., Mr. Contreras, Ryerson, or Lotty often provide protection and care. In *Blood Shot*, when thugs knock out V. I., wrap her in a heavy blanket, and dump her in a lake, Mr. Contreras pulls her out after Peppy finds her.

Especially important is V. I.'s relationship with other women, including her mother, Lotty, and old friends and relatives. As Shuker and Umphries maintain, the "women . . . function as a community, homo social in character and intensity, that mediates Warshawski's relationship to a tough world" (73; see also Pope 159 and Sabine Vanaker 71). In *Blood Shot*, for example, her old childhood friend and basketball teammate Caroline asks V. I. to find out who her unknown father is. After much hesitation, V. I. accepts the request because V. I.'s mother Gabriella often urged her to look after Caroline and because Gabriella defended Caroline's mother Louisa after her parents condemned her and kicked her out because she got pregnant out of wedlock. In *Killing Orders*, Lotty Hershel gets furiously angry because her uncle Stefan has been seriously injured while helping V. I. catch the villainous Archbishop O'Faolin.

Anxious to reconcile her, V. I. says, "Lotty. Lotty, I have been so alone this winter. Do you know the torment I have been through?" (276).

These meaningful friendships and social ties undermine the masculine anomie characterizing Marlowe's or Hammer's relationships. In addition, while Paretsky's novels do not reject, they do qualify the explosive violence that usually characterizes the hard-boiled detective's investigation.[3] In *One Lonely Night*, for example, when Mike Hammer makes the shocking discovery that the fanatic communist Oscar has killed and impersonated Lee, his sane twin brother and a trustworthy conservative politician, Hammer takes pleasure in strangling him: "I laughed while his tongue swelled up and bulged out with his eyes and his face turned black" (176). V. I. also employs such brutal violence, but she often feels regret or disgust, not pleasure. In *Blood Shot*, she shoots and beats the kidnappers of the drugged Louisa, whom they are holding at the Xerxes chemical plant, but her violence and rage sicken her: "Sick of the stench of the plant, of the foulness of the three men, of my own destructive rage. My gorge rose" (326). Moreover, knocking down Mr. Djiak and busting his television set, she rants angrily because she discovers that they kept their daughter Louisa ignorant of sexual matters and then disavowed her when her uncle, known to be sexually abusive, got her pregnant, yet she feels equally disgusted with herself: "I staggered from the house . . . , my stomach heaving, my throat tight and tainted with bile" (277).

Paretsky's fiction also violates the conventional treatment of sex and romance. In *The Girl Hunters*, for example, Hammer says that, when Laura kissed him, "the scalding touch of her tongue . . . worked serpentlike in a passionate orgy that screamed of release" (96). In *Indemnity Only*, V. I. falls asleep relieved that her lover Ralph Devereux did not need any help from her (78). In *Deadlock*, she considers sex with Murray Ryerson a callisthenic activity: "I found out how much exercise my dislocated shoulder was up to" (176). More-over, despite Laura's orgiastic kiss, Hammer feels so little emotional commitment to Laura that at the end he arranges for her to kill herself. By contrast, after her wounded lover Ralph Devereux decides that a relationship with her "just wouldn't work out" (236), a hurt V. I. wishes that she "didn't feel so much like crying" (236). In *Blacklist*, V. I. decides not to make love with her client Dannaugh Graham because loneliness, not love, was her motivation.

While Paretsky's novels subvert the anomic relationships, explosive violence, and intense sexuality of a Philip Marlowe or Mike Hammer, the novels preserve their wise-guy stance. In *The Big Sleep*, when General Sternwood asks Marlowe why Attorney General Wilde fired him, he says, "I test very high on insubordination, General" (10). Similarly, in *Indemnity Only*, when Lt. Mallory asks V. I. why she went to Peter Thayer's apartment, she responds: "I have an instinct for crime. Where evil flourishes, there I will be, on my self-appointed mission to stamp it out" (30). In *Killing Orders*, the police ask her to explain what she is doing in Skokie, Illinois. Reluctant to expose Uncle Stefan's counterfeiting scheme, she responds, "The bagels in Chicago aren't as good as the ones they make out here" (167). Gloria Biamonte rightly says that "V. I.'s self-conscious participation in the rejuvenated genre of detective fiction is . . . highlighted by her penetrating wit" (234).

Although her "penetrating wit" highlights the fiction's conventions, her restrained sexuality, emotional commit-ments, regret at excess violence, and cultivation of friends break with them. So do her conflicts with her clients, friends, and policemen and her uncertainly about her investigations. While Hammer often faces opposition from his traditional ally Pat, his communist enemies, and various city officials, who threaten to jail, arrest, beat, torture, or kill him, he rarely doubts that he has discovered the true criminal or that his killing the criminal represents a just punishment. For instance, in *One Lonely Night*, a judge who condemns Hammer's relentless killing haunts him throughout the novel, but, when he uncovers a brutal communist clique exploiting democratic American freedoms, his self-righteous faith in killing is renewed. As he says, "*The hell of it is, Judge . . . [your] rain of purity has come, and out there in it is the grim specter who is determined that this time he will not miss*" (154).

V. I.'s investigations also produce threats and conflicts, but she often doubts her motives or her method. For example, in *Deadlock*, V. I. investigates the death of her cousin Boom Boom, a retired hockey star who allegedly fell into a lake where the churning propeller of a nearby barge killed him. No one except Lotty Hershel encourages her investigation. When she tells Captain Mallory that Boom Boom was murdered, Mallory urges her to find a husband and take a long vacation. Her family, which always resented Boom Boom's playing professional hockey, suspects that he suffered from depression and committed suicide because his bad knees forced him to give up hockey. When she questions Paige Carrington, Boom Boom's lovely girlfriend, she fears that a traditional female envy may motivate her, as Paige claims. Encouraged by Lotty, she goes ahead, but she suspects that her investigation may show only her sadness and anger at her cousin's untimely death or her jealousy of his lover. Similarly, in *Blood Shot*, Caroline repeatedly asks V. I. to stop trying to discover who Caroline's father was. V. I. refuses, but she fears that her investigation does little more than cause Caroline and her mother Louisa trouble.

Not only does V. I. show an unusual doubt or uncertainty, she is also more emotionally involved than the traditional detective is. In philosophical terms, Paretsky's novels reject the empirical or scientific epistemology of the classical detective novel in which the scientific study of the "facts" reveals the truth about crime and criminals. As Sabine Vanaker says, these novels "posit a subjective, involved, empathic type of knowing different from the objective, distanced knowledge which is the masculine epistemological ideal" (79).

In Paretsky's *Burn Marks* (1990), for example, V. I. aids her peripatetic Aunt Elena after her hotel burns down and, as a result, gets involved in an insurance fraud investigation that uncovers a ruthless clique of policemen, businessmen, and politicians, who include Ralph MacDonald, a billion-aire businessman who burns down her aunt's hotel to make way for a new stadium; Boots Meagher, a shady Democratic party leader trying to stop a progressive alliance of blacks and Hispanics; and Michael Furey, the protégé of Captain Mallory whom Eileen, Mallory's wife, considers the perfect husband for V. I. Justice prevails, yet V. I. engages in many angry rants about the "good" housewife, abused women, possessive or domineering men, and belittled policewomen. At the end, as she drives through the neighborhood in which she, Aunt Elena, Michael, Bobby, Roz, Boots, and her parents grew up, she faults them: "Where they all grew up together and helped each other out because the one thing you must never forget in Chicago is to look out for your own" (336).

In addition to subjective, emotional involvement, such rants show yet another way in which Paretsky's fiction breaks with its generic convention. As Timothy Shuker-Haines and Martha Umphrey suggest, unlike classic detective narratives, which "cleanse society by locating the source of disorder in specific deviant individuals who can be identi-fied and purged," Paretsky's novels "locate society's evils not on the margins but in its most central, stable figures . . . politicians, corporate executives, bankers, union bosses, reli-gious leaders."[4]

Burn Marks extends the liberal ideal of impartial justice to these central figures but preserves this ideal. Moreover, in many detective novels different crimes and investigations come together to reveal a deep, complex crime and justify ideological critique, yet the liberal ideal of impartial justice prevails. In *Farewell, My Lovely*, Marlowe proves that the impoverished Velma is the wealthy Mrs. Grayle and a desperate killer and, as a result, reforms the Oakland police department, getting Red, his unjustly fired pal, reinstated. Similarly, in *Blood Shot*, V. I.'s investigation of Nancy's murder enables her to expose a brutal conspiracy in which the Xerxes chemical plant slowly poisoned its workers and denied them health insurance. Thanks to the notebooks detailing the medical history of Xerxes's employees, V. I. brings to justice Curtis Chigwell, the plant's irresponsible medical officer, Gustave Humboldt, the powerful owner of Xerxes, Steve Dresberg, Chicago's garbage king, and Art Jurshak, the city councilman who provided Humboldt illegal health insurance and killed V. I.'s friend Nancy to conceal it.

By contrast, *Blacklist* (2003) reveals such a deep crime but challenges the ideal. In it, V. I.'s two lines of investigation—the lights at Larchmont Hall and the death of Whitby the black reporter—converge to reveal a complex crime and produce forceful ideological critique. The investigation goes on, however, to uncover the oppressive effects of 1950s McCarthyite anticommunism and post-9/11 repression and, as a result, to question the liberal faith that an impartial detective can establish the truth and restore justice to an unjust world.

In the first investigation, Darraugh Graham hires V. I. to find out why Geraldine Graham, his ninety-one-year-old mother who lives in a retirement facility, sees lights shining at night in Larchmont Hall, her old home. This investigation shows that at Larchmont Hall Catherine Graham, Renee's granddaughter, was concealing Sadawi, an Egyptian dishwasher unjustly suspected of terrorist connections. Since the FBI also suspects that V. I. is concealing Sadawi, the investigation produces forceful, ideological critique. For instance, when the FBI question V. I. about where Sadawi is and what she was doing in Larchmont Hall, she forcefully declares her faith in the Bill of Rights: "If the Bill of Rights is dead, my life, my faith in America, will break" (275). When the FBI say that the Patriot Act allows them to search V. I.'s apartment without a warrant, Mr. Contreras angrily objects that he did not fight in WWII so the government could break into any house that they wanted to (267).

In the second investigation, V. I. tries to find out who killed Marcus Whitby, a distinguished black journalist who was writing an article about the 1930s Federal Negro Theater Project. V. I. figures out that Renee Bayard killed Whitby to protect the reputation of her husband. Whitby had discovered that Calvin Bayard, a successful publisher and liberal opponent of HUAC, betrayed Kylie Ballantine, a prominent black dancer and communist supporter, to Olin Taverner, a HUAC investigator, thereby ruining her career. Unlike Armand Pelletier, a successful left-wing novelist who spent six months in jail and ended up a poor and bitter alcoholic (362) because he refused to name the names of communists, Bayard escaped prosecution and preserved his good reputation not only by betraying Kylie Ballantine but also by threatening to expose the homosexual relationship of Taverner and MacKenzie Graham, Geraldine's husband, who subsequently committed suicide.

The two investigations converge at the end, when, with ninety-year-old Geraldine Graham, V. I. drives to the family's old mountain lodge, where Catherine Graham and Sadawi have fled to escape the police. In a whirlwind ending, Geraldine, injured herself, knocks out Calvin Bayard's wife Renee, who drove there and killed Sadawi. In the usual fashion, V. I. calls Captain Mallory, who arrests Renee for murdering not only Sadawi but also the journalist Whitby and the HUAC investigator Taverner; however, the arrest does not produce the usual justice because the government fears the wealth and influence of Renee, who claims that she killed a "known terrorist" and saved Catherine, and, anxious to shed the blood of possible Muslim terrorists, refuses to prosecute her.

The liberal ideal of justice fails, but the two investigations produce forceful ideological critiques. They imply that the post-9/11 antiterrorism and McCarthyite anticommunism were equally repressive. Moreover, like Mrs. Chigwell, who, after helping V. I. free the drugged Louisa, feels free to travel to Florence by herself and to make her corrupt brother move out of their house, the traditional Geraldine Graham finds her adventures with V. I. liberating. She tells V. I., for instance, that knocking out Renee gave her a pleasure like none she felt before and that she feels, thanks to her adventure with V. I., like a freer spirit than she ever was. To comfort the defeated V. I., Geraldine also says that the good the wealthy do outweighs their evil, but V. I. denies it: "That's pie-in-the-sky stuff, to keep us working stiffs from rising up in fury at the inequities of the world" (457).

Moving beyond the other novels, *Blacklist* critiques political repression and undermines the conventional liberal ideal according to which an independent, impartial detective produces justice. In general, the restrained sexuality, close relationships, uncertain investigations, disgust with violence, and feminist and political rants that Paretsky depicts show that, contrary to the many critics who maintain that detective novels imitate their generic conventions and restate established truths, her novels undermine those conventions and produce forceful and insightful ideological critiques.

Many critics argue, however, that hardboiled mystery novels reject such critiques of their conventions or ideologies.[5] For example, Erin Smith roots the feminist detective fiction of the 1980s and 1990s in the 1930s fiction, in which the hardboiled detective's secretary shows an ambiguous gender—like Mike Hammer's Velda, sexy but often violent too. Smith shows that in the 1920s and 1930s the fiction's largely male, working-class readers acquired only a high-school education. Facing the historic loss of the artisan's economic autonomy, the growth of fast-paced industrial production, and the increased economic independence of women, they pursued middle-class comfort and social mobility, not critiques of genres or ideology. In the 1970s and 1980s, when women's hardboiled fiction grew so explosively popular, its readership had, however, changed dramatically. Now readers include largely college-educated, professional Anglo-American women, who appreciate depictions of strong women and critiques of chauvinism (see Walton and Jones, 22–30, 121–27).

Smith grants that the fiction's generic conventions do not govern the practices of female readers, who, instead of appreciating the plot's complexity or the detective's solution, identify with the protagonist or with minor characters or favor realistic settings in order to work out personal issues or to make sense of a fragmented, complex modern world. As she says, the "ways of reading" of female mystery fans "are a good deal more complex, contradictory, and deeply involved with the personal and institutional histories of writers, publishers, and readers" than textual analysis "could predict" ("Women Readers" 213).[6] She goes on, however, to attribute the fiction's popularity to its advertising because it appeals to women who appreciate independent female professionals and to men who assume that sexy detectives stay "in their place" ("Women Readers" 202). This view assumes that the conditions facing authors and the social practices shaping readers are identical. As Pierre Bourdieu and others argue, such views deny that authors and readers form a field of conflicting interests, groups, and institutions (see *The Rules of Art*). In other words, not only do authors, publishers, reviewers, and advertisers influence readers; so do colleges and universities, which increasingly educate professional women and affect popular taste. Since universities increasingly educate professional women, who now attend college in greater numbers than men do, these educated readers enable the fiction to break down the opposition between formal textual "aesthetics" and the reader's concerns. Because of the readers' increasing sophistication, Paretsky's novels can challenge their enabling conventions and win the appreciation of the reader.

Fredric Jameson also opposes this assimilation of high art and popular culture, but Jameson, who, as I noted in Chapter 1, defends Adorno and Horkheimer's belief that, unlike high art, popular culture supports capitalist commodity production (*Late* 229–31), argues that what he terms the postmodern era effaces the "older (essentially high modernist) frontier between high culture and so-called mass or commercial culture," integrating them both into "commodity production generally." I will discuss this view more fully in the conclusion. For now I should note that, while Jameson grants that the distinction between high art and popular culture, the academic and the ordinary, or the private and the public has broken down, his view of these changes is too negative. He claims that, by breaking down these distinctions, the postmodern era fosters "a whole new wave of American military and economic domination throughout the world" ("Postmodernism" 54–7); however, the changes that have opened detective fiction to critical examination have positive import. Because the reader's gender and sophistication have changed greatly over the last century, detective fiction is no longer restricted to popular or "pulp" magazines and their reviewers; rather, it is studied and taught by literary scholars, who examine and critique the fiction's origins, types, and conventions. In the 1970s and 1980s the humanist opposition to science's domination and the emergence of black studies and black feminism explained and justified the revaluation of *Frankenstein, Huckleberry Finn, Native Son, Light in August,* and *Jazz*; similarly, the growing sophistication of the readers and new academic status of the genre account for and vindicate Paretsky's popularity and her ideological critique. In sum, unlike other detective fiction, Paretsky's novels subvert their generic conventions, produce forceful ideological critique, and achieve popularity because the readers, especially the female readers, have acquired a new sophistication since the genre first emerged in the late nineteenth century and the genre a new ability to straddle the academic world and the marketplace.

FROM AESTHETICS TO READING PRACTICES

THE REINTERPRETATIONS AND REVALUATIONS OF *Franken-stein, Huckleberry Finn, Native Son, Light in August, Jazz,* and Paretsky's fiction show the increased influence and importance of modern reading practices including the humanist opposition to science's domination since the 1960s, the emergence of black studies and black feminism, and the growing sophistication of female readers and the new academic status of popular genres. My argument has been that this account of reading practices overcomes the opposition of aesthetics and socio-historical study. As I suggested in the introduction, since the 1990s some criticism has treated reading as an ethical or pleasurable form of close textual analysis and on that basis rejected the poststructuralist theories and cultural movements of the 1970s and 1980s, Other recent criticism also rejects those theories and movements but defends aesthetic norms in order to restore the autonomy of literature and its centrality in education and social life. Still other recent criticism repudiates aesthetic ideals in order to show that reading reveals the personality or social context of the reader. By contrast, the reading practices I have derived from Foucauldian theory overcomes this opposition of textual or aesthetic ideals and social or historical contexts and situates reading practices in their changing socioeconomic conditions. This theory opens the humanities to those practices, which have, thanks to the modern university's extraordinary growth and importance since at least WWII, acquired an extraordinary cultural influence.

In general, American reading practices have acquired a new importance because the increased influence of the university has broken down the traditional distinctions between aesthetics and commodity production, art and mass media, and private academic discourse and public truth.Critics object, however, that this breakdown means the end of rational debate. As I noted in Chapter 6, Walter Benn Michaels faults Morrison's view of history because it imposes cultural identity and destroys liberal ideals; however, he traces their demise not to the university's new influence but to communism's collapse. As Michaels says, "Only at the end of history could all politics become identity politics" (*Shape* 24). Timothy Brennan also complains that in the postmodern era people engage in a politics of cultural identity, not rational debate about beliefs or class position, but he blames this practice on cold war liberalism, not on its demise. In the 1970s and 1980s it assimilates poststructuralist literary theory and, he says, effectively discredits the left-wing critical theory and radical politics produced by the movement to end the Vietnam War (1–38; see also Jameson, "How Not").

What explains why identity politics excludes "rational" belief is, however, not the collapse nor the resurgence of liberalism but the increased influence of the modern university. This new influence gives American reading practices a new importance but undermines the traditional distinctions between the objective and the subjective, the public and the private, or high and popular art.

The history of these distinctions explains this change. They first emerged in the eighteenth century, when neoclassical humanism was able to unite the aristocracy and the middle classes and to define the educated public or, as Jürgen

Habermas says, the public sphere (see Auerbach 333; Newman 67–87; Parringer 8; and Wellek 1:5–11). In the nineteenth century, the middle classes acquired more power, partisan journals formed diverse publics, and the modern disciplines acquired formal autonomy. As a result, the neoclassical ideal lost its ability to unite the aristocracy and the bourgeoisie and to organize the public sphere;[1] nonetheless, in the late nineteenth century, when universities established departments of languages and literature, the scientific philologists, who preserved the "public" neoclassical notion of generic types and biographical and historical contexts, dominated because in the late eighteenth and early nineteenth centuries education turned popular as diverse institutions and organizations sought to regulate the health and the welfare of the population by, among other methods, educating them (See Hunter 183–84).

The philological method remained central until the 1940s and 1950s, when literary study acquired the graduate programs, distinct fields, and professional associations and fostered formal methods and specialized research (Guillory, "Literary Study" 32–36). At that time, the expanding Anglo-American university absorbed avant-garde artists and liberal intellectuals, making their work more influential but exacerbating the conflict of high and popular art and the furthering the limitations of the public sphere.

As I noted, after World War II the New Critics, who dominated American English departments at that time and later, promoted the modernist avant-garde and dismissed popular culture as well as the neoclassical humanists and generalists committed to the public sphere (Graff 14). Similarly, the New York Intellectuals allied themselves with the dominant formal critics, turning high modern art into what Lionel Trilling called "a polemical concept" and rejecting popular liberal and democratic writers (see Trilling, *Liberal* 277–87).

As Chapter 1 indicated, Adorno, Horkheimer, and other theorists of the Frankfurt School also claimed that Enlightenment science dominates and dehumanizes social life but that high art resists this domination. More recently, Jameson has extended this view, claiming that capitalism produces reified institutions that high art resists, as Adorno says, but that in the postmodern era capitalism dominates external and internal nature, social practices, and the mind. Moreover, he traces this all-encompassing reification not to the instrumental rationality characterizing the enlightenment era but to what he terms the fragmented subject peculiar to the modernist and postmodernist periods (*Late* 229–31).

Other theorists grant that the reified institutions of postmodern society fragment the subject, which, as Jameson claims, divides into public and private, rational and emotional, or objective and subjective selves, but they argue that postmodern art still resists its commodified character and subverts established ideologies and stereotypes.[2] Still other theorists deny that popular culture dupes ordinary people as easily as Jameson and the Frankfurt School claim, but many of these theorists also fear that the specialized disciplines are reified or elitist and that modern culture is fragmented and in decline.[3] In other words, a broad range of critics, including the New Critics, the New York intellectuals, Jameson, the Frankfurt School, aesthetic or textual critics, and some postmodernists have justified the subversive force of modern high art and dismissed popular or "mass" art; academic criticism; and black, women's, gay, and other programs and movements because they oppose capitalist commodity production, the reified disciplines, abstract theories, or the fragmentation and decline of public sphere (Howe, *Notebook* 128; see also Huyssen 26; Norris 242; Pietz 65; Andrew Ross 42–64; Schaub 17; and Sinfield 102).

Foucauldian theory grants that in the postmodern era the division of high art and popular culture or the university and the public sphere breaks down, and the world of commodity production has integrated high art into its spheres. Frow shows, for example, that what he terms the "postmodernization of the economy" includes the assimilation of aesthetics into commodity production, but he argues that scholars who like Jameson oppose this integration mistakenly deduce postmodern cultural practices from postmodern economic processes (*Time* 49-61).

He also suggests that Foucauldian theory rejects such a reductive view of culture and establishes the positive import of cultural institutions, including the university. In other words, the university's new influence makes reading practices a positive force rather than a litany of evils ranging from the spread of irrational cultural identities and the loss of firm beliefs to the neglect of ideological or economic divisions and the fragmentation of the subject. It is true that since the 1980s and 1990s corporate elites increasingly dominate the privatized university because in the "post-Fordist" economy American industry and finance have shifted to third world countries and conservative federal and state governments have greatly reduced their financial support. Higher education, which now educates over 55 percent of young adults, has, nonetheless, grown more important. Although the reading practices do not escape from the breakdown or fragmentation of public and private spheres, they can, as a result, justify the humanist, black, women's, and multicultural movements and programs that have revalued and reinterpreted *Frankenstein*, Sara Paretsky's detective fiction, *Native Son, Light in August, Jazz*, and *The Adventures of Huckleberry Finn*, to mention only those few novels that I have discussed, and that, along with traditional fields and studies, make up cultural study in the twenty-first century.

Notes

CHAPTER 1

1. See Eagleton, *The Ideology* 334–35 and 354–55; Jameson, *Late* 248–49; Armstrong 175; Malpas 13–15; and Zwiarek 53. For the last ten years alone, the MLA bibliography lists over 450 articles on Adorno's aesthetics.

2. For accounts that defend Adorno's aesthetics and repudiate poststructuralist theory, see Eagleton, *Ideology* 353–55; Jameson, *Late* 9, 31; and Pensky, 6. For antiaesthetic versions of Foucault, see Fish, "Consequences" 437; Mailloux, *Histories* 57; and Bennett, *Outside* 143–67.

3. See also Brennan, who says that the importance of Heidegger stems from "his self-appointed role as historical foil to the Hegelian left" (16).

4. See also Habermas, who says, "As opposed as the intentions behind their respective philosophies of history are, Adorno is in the end very similar to Heidegger as regards his position on the theoretical claims of objectivating thought and reflection" (385). For thorough discussions of these similarities, see Dallmayr, Roberts, Wenning, and Ziarek For a dismissal of these similarities, see *Late Marxism*, where Jameson says, "I have been surprised by the increasing frequency of comparisons with his arch-enemy Heidegger (whose philosophy, he once observed, 'is fascist to its innermost core')" (9).

5. See Feenberg, who says that "Adorno himself acknowledged that Lukács's concept of reification" led to the Frankfurt School's modern view of capitalism (165).

6. *Ideology* 353–55; more negative, Jameson says that, while Derrida accepts liberal ideals and rejects any representation of the real, Adorno's "revolutionary" theories emphasize "the presence of late capitalism as a totality within the very forms of our concepts or of the works of art themselves" (*Late* 9, 31). See also Pensky 6.

7. Deleuze says that Foucault reads Heidegger through Nietzsche: the will to power explains the ability of discourse to bring what is into the open or the clearing where it becomes visible even as it recedes into darkness (120).

8. Of the Frankfurt School, Foucault says, for example, that "in their history men have never ceased to constitute themselves, that is to say, to displace continually their subjectivity, to constitute themselves in a multiple and infinite series of different subjectivities . . . it is there that there is an incompatibility with the Frankfurt School" (*Dits*, 5:75, my translation). The critique of the onto-theological tradition is fully argued in Paul Allen Miller 54–74.

9. This disagreement has a long history. It is well known that Derrida faulted Foucault's claim that in the *Meditations*, Rene Descartes maintains that, to achieve certainty, reason excludes madness but not dreaming. Derrida objects that the certainty in terms of which Descartes explains rational thought includes both madness and dreaming. He writes, "Madness is only a particular case, and, moreover, not the most serious one, of the sensory illusion which interests Descartes at this point" (*Writing* 50). Derrida goes on to argue that, because of the evil deceiver, who can render even our simple and universal ideas illusions, Descartes maintains that, far from excluding madness, reason accepts it. In a response written ten years later, Foucault defends both his claim that Descartes excludes madness but not dreaming. He argues that Derrida examines only the formal terms of Descartes's text, not the historical episteme of Descartes's era. The episteme gives his Latinate term for madness and the status of his meditation a special weight which Derrida overlooks. The Latin term identifies madness with insanity, which, according to French law, denied a person was responsible. A meditation does not only follow formal rules of proof; a meditation also modifies the subject, but insanity would render him or her incapable of rational modification. Moreover, since Derrida finds in the absences and oppositions of the text the classical origins of the western philosophical tradition, Foucault considers him "the most decisive modern representative" of a "system" or "old tradition," which textualizes "discursive practices."

CHAPTER 2

1. See also *The Range of Interpretation*, where Iser argues that, like the interplay of the fictive and the imaginary, cultural translation or interpretation explains the practices of psychological, sociological, and theological systems and, by envisaging new possibilities, exposes their limits and transcends them.

2. David Cousins Hoy says, "Fish's theory is . . . akin to philosophical hermeneutics in its insistence that the literary work only comes to be in a process of understanding and interpretation" (155).

3. See Bennett's *Marxism* 42–43 and Frow's *Marxism* 101–2. In *Formalism and Marxism*'s second edition, Bennett says that Bakhtin's theories of discourse would provide a better account of reading than those of the Russian formalists did. The Bakhtin "that has emerged . . . is a more complex one, far richer theoretically and with a more nuanced and ambivalent in relation to Marxist thought than I had appreciated" (144).

CHAPTER 3

1. See Menegaldo's "Introduction," which says, "For a long time the novel was associated with gothic stories, a popular but minor genre, the author being accused of cultivating strong sensations, of exciting terror and horror instead of morality and propriety. Recall the polemic concerning the 'paternity' of the text: according to certain critiques, Mary Shelley would have been only a medium, profiting from an exceptional literary entourage or a narrow collaboration with her husband, the poet Shelley who revised the original manuscript carefully. . . . The novel is sometimes still judged too long, too wordy, didactic to excess or melodramatic. One stigmatizes its lack of unity, the hybrid character of its structure; one underlines the improbabilities of the plot; one minimizes the originality of a story overcharged with literary influences. The monstrosity of the creature is sometimes assimilated to that of a composite, heterogeneous text, which borrows from multiple genres without arriving at a unity of effect" (3; my translation).
2. Levine and Knoepflmacher xiii. See also Marcus, "*Frankenstein*," which says that "only in the last twenty-five years or so has it entered fully and actively been deliberately enlisted and impressed into the academic canon" (151), and Schoene-Harwood 22.
3. See also Hammond, who says that in *Frankenstein* "Mary Wollstonecraft Shelley provided those of us who expect to live into the twenty-first century with a powerful metaphor for many of the scientific dilemmas we must face" (8), and Vaguin 155–56.
4. Schoene-Harwood 8; see also Botting 3–4.
5. See Davidson and Goldberg, who says that "[w]ith increasing institutional dominance by technology, applied science, and the professions, the humanities' seat at the academic table has grown shabby, to say the least" (42–43). See also Guillory, who says that "antagonism to science is not an expression of Ludditism . . . but rather a response of the cultural disciplines" to science's "triumph" in the "twentieth-century university ("The Sokal Affair" 479–80).

6. See also Aldiss and Jones, who consider it the founding paradigm of science fiction.

7. For instance, in 1926 Edward Coote Pinkney said, "That Mrs. Shelley was its author, we do not believe: on collating the novels supposed to be hers, with the poems of her husband, it becomes apparent that they are the offspring of one brain; nor do we think (without intending the slightest disrespect to the better half of the human race) that a woman could have composed the work in question" (192–93). For a contrary view, see Mellor, who has shown that Percy Shelley's revisions of the 1818 edition did little more than make Mary Shelley's diction more Latinate (*Shelley* 219–24; see also Robinson). See also MacCarthy, who in 1947 condemned the novel's structure: its "most glaring fault . . . is due to the fact that, having begun 'It was on a dreary night in November'; Mrs. Shelley later inserted four prefatory chapters."

8. See Williams 125–72 and Altick 30–77. See also Ross, who says that eighteenth-century educators working in dissenting academies or secondary schools taught their students that, "the true pleasures of reading could only come in relation to texts of an intellectually demanding nature" (225). These educators claimed, moreover, that novels, which one could consume "too easily and rapidly," had "injurious effects."

9. See Flint, who shows that in the Renaissance it "was clearly stated that women should not choose their own reading material; and that it should be chosen for them with care. . . . The patterns of reasoning which lay behind Renaissance prescriptive remarks concerning woman's reading were remarkably close, in outline, to ones which were repeated during the next three centuries, linking together preoccupations with bodily and mental fitness. Whilst too great an acquaintance with light reading might lead her sexually astray, either in imagination or reality, it would also distract her from developing intellectually and spiritually" (22–23).

10. See Brantlinger 26–34; Ferris 35–52; and Pearson 170–75.

11. See Brantlinger 59–60; Pearson 178–80, and Baldick 48–67.

12. See Pearson, who says that this novel "not only laughs at its heroine's uncritical addiction to Gothic fiction," it also uses this addiction, what Pearson calls "the female quixote plot," "as a smokescreen behind which to launch a vigorous defense of the novel in general, and women writers in particular" (210).

13. For a fine account of the importance which Austen's work acquired in nineteenth-century circulating libraries, see Benedict 63–86.

14. Lewes 15.

15. Cited in Southam 225.

16. Forry points out that in 1823 *Presumption, or, The Fate of Frankenstein* "enjoyed enormous popularity, being performed thirty-seven times in its first season" (3). From 1823 to 1826, at least fifteen dramas employed characters and themes from Shelley's novel. By 1990 there were over ninety dramatic productions (Forry ix) as well as many movie versions, television shows, commercials, and even comic books.

17. Anon. Review of *Presumption; or, the Fate of Frankenstein. London Morning Post* 30 July 1823. Cited in Wolfson 327.

18. Benita suggests that "Victor Frankenstein's wholly masculine endeavour . . . has become an enduring metaphor for the various productions of technoscience which have been proved less benign than their intended purpose, as well as for the productions of 'big science' which exploit natural resources and whole populations in a cynical appropriation of profit" (5).

19. See Rose, "Custody Battles" 810 and Schoene-Harwood 11.

20. Some of them grant that Victor Frankenstein is an overreacher, as traditional critics say, but, defending a women's literary tradition or nineteenth-century notions of feminine propriety, they argue that what explains the depiction of the monster is Shelley's experience of motherhood and of the orphan's life (Moers), her repressed feminist rage (Gilbert and Gubar), or her traditional female distrust of self-assertion, including imaginative activity and trust in nature (Poovey). Other feminists argue that the novel critiques the family's narrow, incestuous norms of gratitude and obligation (Mellor), or that Victor's destruction of the unfinished female monster means that his racist and misogynist fears of third-world women preclude sexual reproduction (Spivak).

21. See, for example, Guillory, "The Sokal Affair" 479–86; Messer-Davidow 213; and Wiegman 142.

CHAPTER 5

1. Critics who consider the novel protest fiction and implicitly or explicitly deny the existential or modernist character of Bigger include Bell 166; Bone 151; Burgum 121; Davis, Jr., cited in Reilly, *Reception* 75; DeCoste 141 and 143; Foley, *Politics* 95–96; Hynes 96; Margolies 72; and Siegel 97. Critics who treat the novel as an account of Bigger's liberation and deny or minimize its protest of class and racial oppression include Baker, "Introduction" 5; Bayliss 5; Butler 55; Fishburn 90; George 504; Gibson; Joyce 24–25 and 103–4; JanMohamed 84–85; and Kennedy 283.

2. See also Bryant, who claims that "Bigger is . . . psychologically free in a way that even Max is not . . . Max's failure suggests that the Communist party, like Mrs. Dalton, like Bigger's family, is blind, too" (24); Hakutani, who appreciates the novel's protest against racial discrimination (61) as well as Max's enabling Bigger to grow (83); Howe, who says, "Between Wright's feelings as a Negro and his beliefs as a Communist there is hardly a genuine fusion" (139); Skerrett, who says that the last section presents "an open-ended or suspended argument in which Wright is refusing to allow Bigger's individuality to be swallowed up or subsumed by Max's social analyses" (37); Stepto, who says that Max, not Bigger, proves articulate and sensitive, but Bigger is clearly the hero ("Wright" 64–65), and Reilly, who says that, while the novel justifies Max's social analyses, Bigger finds his own voice ("Giving" 58–59).

3. Theodore Dreiser, a fellow member of the Anti-Fascist League of American Writers and other left-wing writers' associations, was one of Wright's favorite writers (see Rowley 60 and 87). Reviewers who note the parallels of *Native Son* and *An American Tragedy* include Howard Mumford Jones, *The Boston Evening Transcript* (March 2, 1940); Clifton Fadiman, *New Yorker*, 16 (March 2, 1940); Peter Monro Jack, *New York Times Book Review* (March 3, 1940); Edward Skillin, Jr., *Commonweal*, 31 (March 8, 1940); *The Chicago Defender* (March 16, 1940); Ben Davis, Jr. (New York) *Sunday Worker* (April 14, 1940); Samuel Sillen, *New Masses*, 35 (April 30, 1940); and Sterling A. Brown, *Opportunity*, 18 (June 1940). They are reprinted in Reilly 47, 48–49, 53, 63, 64 69, 84, and 96, respectively. Critics who consider Dreiser's fiction an important influence include Ellison, who says that the work of Dreiser and Upton Sinclair developed "techniques for grappling with the deeper American realities" (in Gates and Appiah 14); Burgum, who notes that Wright follows the "general plan" of *An American Tragedy* until the trial scene, where he merges his personality with Max (121–22); Howe, who says that the novel shows the "molding influence of Theodore Dreiser, especially the Dreiser of *An American Tragedy*" ("Black Boys" 138; Fabre, who considers the parallels of Dreiser and Wright biographical as well as literary ("Beyond" 41–42); Foley, whose detailed comparison of *An American Tragedy* and *Native Son* is one of the best ("Politics" 191–94); Stepto, who examines why Wright turns to Dreiser or Sinclair Lewis and not black authors ("I Thought" 61–62); and Hakutani, who examines in detail how the two novels diverge (84–99).

4. See Hakutani, who argues that, "despite the obvious parallels between *Native Son* and *An American Tragedy*, the comparison is of limited value"

because, unlike Clyde, who, defeated at the end, never gains any insight into himself or his position, Bigger achieves liberation (86–88).

5. Fabre points out that, in 1938, when Wright was writing the novel, his friend Jane Newton convinced him to reread "with close attention to technique and detail *The Possessed* and *The Brothers Karamazov*" (*Books* 170). As a result, he came to appreciate Dostoievsky's existentialism, so much so that, when Newton objected to Bigger's killing his girlfriend Bessie Mears, Wright defended the killing on the grounds that, as Fabre says, Bigger was "gradually turning into another Raskolnikov" (171).

6. For a discussion of these parallels, see Cooke 87–88, and Portelli 260.

7. Lee says, "Throughout the Depression years and even into the 1940s [Wright] was regularly taken to reflect the Communist Party view that Marxism pointed a way 'beyond race' . . . Then, during the Eisenhower Tranquil '50s, . . . he found himself castigated as some kind of literary dissident, an ungrateful black anti-American voice . . . still enamoured of Soviet Russia . . . In turn, in the 1960s, . . . the generation raised on Civil Rights and then marches like that into Selma and inner-city explosions and the rhetoric of Malcolm X and the Panthers seized on him as an exemplary spokesman for Black Power, an early standard-bearer of either-or black militancy" (111).

8. See Gates and Appiah, *Hurston* 17. Wright also faults the "minstrel fashion" in which the novel entertains white readers (17). In the more moderate *Negro Voices in American Fiction* (1948), Gloster praises the novel's "vivid pictures of social life in Eatonville, gambling dives in Jacksonville, and bean-picking communities in the Everglades" and "the social tension of the Southern scene," but he too complains that Hurston is "more interested in folklore and dialect than in social criticism"(237). As late as 1973, Turner, who treats the novel as a bad classical tragedy because it mixes the comic and the serious, lamented "Miss Hurston's continued emphasis upon intraracial and intrafamilial hatred" (108).

9. See also Scruggs, who argues that Bigger, whose life was "one long act of rebellion against what society officially considers pious" (166), deserves the electric chair and that, far from atheistic communism, Wright describes Chicago in biblical terms. "If Max gives his redeemed city a Marxist bias, Wright makes sure that readers see it in a more universal light through its archetypal setting" (168).

10. See Foley, "Marxism" 5–37; and Joyce, "Black Woman" 543–65. See also Michaels, who also says that Wright situates Bigger outside black culture (*Our America* 126), but, more negative than Foley or Joyce, claims that multicultural critics who, like Baker, treat race as a legitimate category are themselves racist.

11. See also Christian, who says, because of these theorists, "some of our most daring and potentially radical critics (and by *our* I mean black, women, third world) have been influenced, even co-opted, into speaking a language and defining their discussion in terms alien to and opposed to our needs and orientation" ("Race" 52).

12. Similarly, Barbara Herrnstein Smith says that a text may be rediscovered as an "unjustly neglected masterpiece" when "different of its properties and possible functions become foregrounded by a new set of subjects with emergent interests and purposes" ("Contingencies" 1341).

13. For a full discussion of these polemics, see Goldstein 17–20.

14. As Lauter says, a democratic humanities is "a goal of both progressive faculty and working class, minority, and immigrant communities, and thus an intellectual and policy basis for alliances between such groups" (63).

CHAPTER 6

1. Weinstein recognizes that "Morrison . . . refuses the plot of tragic impasse to which modernist forms tend to lead Faulkner" (178) but considers it just another sign of their different "cultural positioning." Bloom considers "the ideologies of political correctness" . . . "deeply embedded in *Beloved*" (Intro., 2). Other critics assume that the similar themes or subjects of Faulkner and Morrison show their aesthetic transcendence. For example, Denard says that Faulkner and Morrison both depict those "other" Americans, those whom Morrison calls the "discredited": "For Faulkner, the discredited are the defeated southern whites . . . Morrison's discredited are American blacks, with slave and sharecropper pasts." The "great merit" of Faulkner and Morrison's work is that they embue their subjects with a mythical "import and still . . . question, transform, and enlarge the mythical tradition to which they believe all history is connected" (21–22). Duval says that Faulkner and Morrison both treat outsiders; oral, blues, and folk traditions; and miscegenation, racism, or "colorism" ("Anxiety" 9–13). Kodat says that "*Absalom, Absalom!* and *Beloved* not only represent African American history artistically: they comment upon the history of artistically representing African Americans." Hogan focuses "upon Sutpen's mansion and 124 as fictional manifestations of Lincoln's American 'house'" and reads "both houses as spaces defined by individual and communal identity as well as by gender" (168).

2. Novak says, for example, that these novels present themselves as generic and psychological types: "a ghost story, a murder mystery, and a process

of psychotherapy—perhaps even of exorcism—carried out at the cultural level" (206).

3. Accounts which emphasize the novel's African American contexts include, in addition to Burton, Carmean, Grewal, Mbalia, and Rodrigues. Those which emphasize the novel's postmodern subversion of literary conventions include, in addition to Rubenstein, Duvall; Gates, "Review"; Peach; and Tally.

4. Similarly, Barbara Smith says that a text may be rediscovered as an "unjustly neglected masterpiece" when "different of its properties and possible functions become foregrounded by a new set of subjects with emergent interests and purposes" ("Contingencies" 1341).

5. See McKay, "Intro" 5. Ohmanns says that Random House publications were much more likely than other publications to be reviewed in *The New York Times Book Review* or some other prestigious review or magazine. Moreover, a novel that, thanks to Random House's extraordinary influence, has been positively reviewed is "likely to draw the attention of academic critics in more specialized academic journals . . . and by this route make its way into college curricula, where the very context—course title, academic setting, methodology—gave it de facto recognition as literature" (75). Ohmanns adds that the "college classroom and the academic journal have become in our society the final arbiters of literary merit, and even of survival. It is hard to think of a novel more than twenty-five years old . . . that still commands a large readership outside of school and college" (75).

6. Michaels sharply distinguishes rational disputes about ideology, ownership, or class position from the subjective recognition of identity ("what people are"), but the cold war disputes also posed questions of identity, including the (in)famous question, "Are you now or have you ever been a communist?"

CHAPTER 7

1. See also Erin Smith, who says that the feminist detective fiction of the 1980s and 1990s is implicit in the 1930s fiction, in which the detective's secretary shows an ambiguous gender—like Mike Hammer's Velda, sexy but often violent too (*Hard-Boiled: Working-Class Readers and Pulp Magazines*).

2. I use the term "liberal" to denote the Enlightenment belief that, to establish the truth or justice, an individual does not accept or defend established traditions; an individual preserves his or her individual autonomy and objectivity and examines the facts in a neutral or unbiased

manner. Unlike modern positivist or analytic philosophy, which reduces ideals to individual preferences, the classical empiricism of John Locke, David Hume, and others brings together this Enlightenment view of objectivity and middle-class ideals of justice or virtue; however, while Hume analyzed complex terms, detectives like Holmes or Poirot engage in the factual analysis of concrete contexts. Longhurst, who associates this method with the liberal "Victorian sense of scientific, industrial, and technological 'progress,'" rightly says that Conan Doyle effectively negotiated a transference" of this empirical method "to the domain of society" (55). Subsequent discussion will challenge this method, which feminists like Carol Gilligan identify with a male perspective, as well as the middle-class ideal of justice.

3. Vanaker says that "Paretsky is aware of sinister, anti-feminist, and even fascist qualities within the make-up of her detective protagonist" (67).

4. 77; For a contrary view, see Bertens and H'haen, who complain that Warshawski shows an "almost paranoid suspicion of 'the system'" that "rules out any sort of political solution to the various social problems she encounters in the course of her adventures" (37).

5. Some critics emphasize the differences between classical British mysteries and the hardboiled detective. Other critics argue that the conventions of detective fiction may include not only gentlemanly amateurs like Poe's Dupin or Doyle's Holmes or hardboiled cynics like Chandler's Marlowe but also the resourceful tricksters, heroes, and chivalrous knights of classical narratives and medieval romances (see Docker, 219–25, and Plain, 4–5). Despite these differences, these critics claim that detective fiction does not allow ideological critique (see Cawelti 95–98, Docker 221, and Ebert 14.

6. See also Hermes, who also belittles interpretations based on generic conventions or textual practices and interviews and analyzes contemporary readers of women's detective fiction.

CONCLUSION

1. See Auerbach 333, and Chartier 71–108. Other scholars have suggested that, instituted in the public schools, where Matthew Arnold was chief inspector for twenty years, this humanism stifled the rebellion and the opposition of women and the working class, imposed bourgeois forms of national unity, and, by the 1880s and 1890s, adopted racist and antisemitic tones. See Baldick 82; Doyle 12; Bernal 1:347–66; and Graff 13. See also *The Order of Things*, where Foucault shows that the breakdown of humanism enables the disciplines to acquire a formal autonomy

contrary to humanist ideals. He says that in the nineteenth century the study of the familiar philology, biology, and political economy replaced the eighteenth century's strange study of language, riches, and history. Knowledge has not grasped its objects more precisely or uncovered new objects; it has acquired new figures—production, life, language. Foucault shows that, at the same time, nineteenth century disciplines developed an opposition between positive knowledge and transcendental critique. On the one side, the forms of rationality detached and reattached themselves to the positive disciplines; on the other, transcendental philosophy subjected the disciplines to critique, exposing the subjectivity, finitude, and being of the knower. In this way the nineteenth-century episteme invented the figure of man, whom the eighteenth century did not discuss. In the twentieth century, however, the modern episteme, which broke into the mathematical sciences, the social sciences, and philosophical disciplines, subverted the human figure grounding the nineteenth century disciplines and allowed them to establish their formal autonomy.

2. See, for example, Spanos, who considers the "anti-detective" story the "paradigmatic literary archetype" of the postmodern imagination, suggests such stories violently frustrate the "programmed expectations" of the detective drama series, including those expectations which find their "fulfillment in the imposed and habituating certainties of the well-made world of the corporate and totalitarian states" (24–25; see also Tani 46).

3. For example, Waugh maintains that postmodern culture subverts the traditional aesthetic foundations of high art and in a democratic way accommodates the practices of popular culture and modern social life; at the same time, she defends the oppositional force of postmodernism: "Instead of defending Postmodernism as an authentic response to the exhaustion of other modes of art or knowledge or attacking it as an inauthentic capitulation to commercial culture, why not see it as an attempt to *modify* the past . . . in the light of a present in which recognition of the pervasiveness of consumer culture is not, necessarily, total capitulation to it" (61). See also Collins, who argues that popular detective fiction critiques its own ideological distinctions and establishes its own discursive realm with its own sense of justice; Easthope, who complains that in the Frankfurt School's account of popular culture dupes ordinary readers into enjoying it (79); and Brantlinger, who says that "art or high culture is no more radical or liberating in and of itself than is commodified mass culture" (*Crusoe's Footprints* 196).

WORKS CITED

Adams, Richard P. *Faulkner: Myth and Motion*. Princeton, NJ: Princeton UP, 1968.

Adorno, Theodor. *Aesthetic Theory*. Trans. C. Lenhardt. New York: Routledge, 1984.

Adorno, Theodor, and Max Horkheimer. *Dialectic of Enlightenment*. Trans. John Cumming. 1944. New York: Continuum, 1972.

Aldiss, Brian W. and David Wingrove. *Trillion Year Spree: The History of Science Fiction*. London: Victor Gollancz, 1986.

Algeo, Ann M. *The Courtroom as Forum: Homicide Trials by Dreiser, Wright, Capote, and Mailer*. New York: Peter Lang, 1996.

Altick, Richard D. *The English Common Reader: A Social History of the Mass Reading Public, 1800–1900*. Chicago: U of Chicago P, 1957.

Anon. Review of *Frankenstein or The Modern Prometheus*. *The British Critic* n.s., 9 (April 1818): 432–438. 18 March 2004 <http://www.rc.umd.edu/reference/mschronology/reviews.html>

Anon. Review of *Frankenstein or The Modern Prometheus*. *The Edinburgh Magazine and Literary Miscellany: A New Series of* "The Scots Magazine" 2 (March 1818). Cited in *Mary Shelly Frankenstein*. Ed. Paul J. Hunter. New York: Norton, 1996. 191–96.

Arac, Jonathan. Huckleberry Finn *as Idol and Target: The Functions of Criticism in Our Time*. Madison: U of Wisconsin P, 1997

Armstrong, Isabel. *The Radical Aesthetic*. Oxford: Blackwell, 2000.

Auerbach, Erich. *Literary Language and Its Public in Late Latin Antiquity and in the Middle Ages*. Trans. Ralph Manheim. 1958. Princeton, NJ: Princeton UP, 1993.

Austen, Jane. *Northanger Abbey*. New York: New American Library, 1965.

Awkward, Michael. *Inspiriting Influences: Tradition, Revision, and Afro-American Women's Novels*. New York: Columbia UP, 1989.

Backman, Melvin. *"Absalom, Absalom!" Twentieth Century Interpretations of* Absalom, Absalom! Ed. Arnold Goldman. Englewood Cliffs, NJ: Prentice-Hall, 1971. 59–75.

Baetzhold, Howard. "Mark Twain and Dickens; Why the Denial?" *Dickens Studies Annual* 16 (1987): 189–219.

Baker, Houston A., Jr. *Blues, Ideology, and Afro-American Literature: A Vernacular Theory*. Chicago: U of Chicago P, 1984.

————. "Introduction." *Twentieth Century Interpretations of* Native Son: *A Collection of Critical Essays*. Ed. Houston A. Baker, Jr. Englewood Cliffs, NJ: Prentice, 1972. 1–20.

Baldick, Chris. "The Politics of Monstrosity." *Frankenstein: Mary Shelley*. Ed. Fred Botting. London: MacMillan Press, 1995. 48–67.

Barnett, Pamela E. "Figurations of Rape and the Supernatural in *Beloved*." *Toni Morrison's* Beloved. Ed. Harold Bloom. Philadelphia: Chelsea House, 1999. 193–205

Bayliss, John F. "*Native Son*: Protest or Psychological Study?" *Negro American Literature Forum* 1 (Fall 1967): 5–6.

Belenky, Mary Field. *Women's Ways of Knowing: The Development of Self, Voice, and Mind*. New York: Basic Books, 1986.

Bell, Bernard W. "*Beloved*: A Womanist Neo-Slave Narrative; or Multivocal Remembrances of Things Past." *Toni Morrison's* Beloved. Ed. Harold Bloom. Philadelphia: Chelsea House, 1999. 57–68.

————. *The Afro-American Novel and Its Tradition*. Amherst: U of Massachusetts P, 1987.

————. "Twain's 'Nigger' Jim: The Tragic Face behind the Minstrel Mask." *Satire or Evasion? Black Perspectives on* Huckleberry Finn. Ed. James S. Leonard, Thomas A. Tenney, and Thadious M. Davis. Durham, NC: Duke UP, 1992. 124–40.

Benedict, Barbara M. "Sensibility by the Numbers: Austen's Work as Regency Popular Fiction," *Janeites: Austen's Disciples and Devotees*. Ed. Deidre Lynch. Princeton, NJ: Princeton UP, 2000. 63–86.

Benita, Debra. *Women, Science and Fiction: The Frankenstein Inheritance*. New York: Palgrave, 2000.

Bennett, Tony. *Culture: A Reformer's Science*. St. Leonards, Australia: Allyn & Unwin, 1998.

————. *Formalism and Marxism*. London: Methuen & Co., 1979.

————. *Outside Literature*. New York: Routledge, 1990.

Berland, Alwyn. Light in August: *A Study in Black and White*. New York: Twayne Publishers, 1992.

Bernstein, J. M. *The Fate of Art: Aesthetic Alienation from Kant to Derrida and Adorno*. University Park: Pennsylvania State UP, 1992.

————. *The Philosophy of the Novel: Lukács, Marxism, and the Dialectics of Form*. Minneapolis: U of Minnesota P, 1984.

Bernstein, Richard J. "The Rage against Reason." *Philosophy and Literature*, 10.2 (1986): 186–210.

Bertens, Hans, and Theo H'haen. *Contemporary American Crime Fiction*. New York: Palgrave, 2001.

Bérubé, Michael. "Introduction: Engaging the Aesthetic." *The Aesthetics of Cultural Studies*. Ed. Michael Bérubé. Oxford: Blackwell, 2005. 1–27.

Biamonte, Gloria A. "Funny Isn't It? Testing the Boundaries of Gender and Genre in Women's Detective Fiction." *Look Who's Laughing: Gender and Comedy*. Ed. Gail Finney. Langhorne, PA: Gordon and Breach, 1994. 231–54.

Blair, Walter. *Mark Twain and Huck Finn*. Berkeley: U of California P, 1973

Bleich, David. "Gender Interests in Reading and Language." *Gender and Reading:Essays on Readers, Texts, and Contexts*. Ed. Elizabeth A. Flynn and Patrocinio Schweickart. Baltimore: Johns Hopkins UP, l986. 286–313.

———. "What Literature is 'Ours'?" *Reading Sites: Social Difference and Reader Response*. Ed. Patrocinio P. Schweikart and Elizabeth A. Flynn. New York: Modern Language Association of America, 2004. 286–313.

Bleikasten, André. "Fathers in Faulkner." *The Fictional Father: Lacanian Readings of the Text*. Ed. Robert Con Davis. Amherst: U of Massachusetts P, 1981. 115–46.

———. "*Light in August*: The Closed Society and its Subjects." *New Essays on* Light in August. Ed.by Michael Millgate. Cambridge: Cambridge UP, 1987: 81–102.

Bloom, Allan. *The Closing of the American Mind: How Higher Education Has Failed Democracy and Impoverished the Souls of Today's Students*. New York: Simon & Schuster, 1987.

Bloom, Harold. *How to read and why*. New York: Scribner, 2000.

———. Introduction. *Toni Morrison's Beloved*. Ed. Harold Bloom. Philadelphia: Chelsea House Publishers, 1999: 1–3.

Bone, Robert A. *The Negro Novel in America*. New Haven, CT: Yale UP, 1958.

"Born to Trouble: *The Adventures of Huck Finn*." *Culture Shock: Series & Beyond*. February 12, 2000. <http://www.pbs.org/wgbh/cultureshock/flashpoints/literature/huck.html>

Botting, Fred. *Making Monstrous*: Frankenstein, *Criticism, Theory*. Manchester: Manchester UP, 1991.

Bourdieu, Pierre. *The Rules of Art: Genesis and Structure of the Literary Field*. Trans. Susan Emanuel. Cambridge: Polity, 1996.

Bové, Paul. *In the Wake of THEORY*. Hanover, NH: Wesleyan UP, 1992.

Brantlinger, Patrick. *Crusoe's Footprints: Cultural Studies in Britain and America*. New York: Routledge, 1990.

———. *The Reading Lesson: The Threat of Mass Literacy in Nineteenth-Century British Fiction*. Bloomington: Indiana UP, 1998.

———. *Who Killed Shakespeare? What's Happened to English since the Radical Sixties*. New York: Routledge, 2001.

Brooks, Cleanth. *William Faulkner: The Yoknapatawpha Country*. New Haven, CT: Yale UP, 1963.

Brunkhorst, Hauke, "Irreconcilable Modernity: Adorno's Aesthetic Experimentalism and the Transgression Theorem." *The Actuality of Adorno: Critical Essays on Adorno and the Postmodern.* Ed. Max Pensky. Albany: SUNY P, 1997. 43–61.

Bryant, Jerry H. "The Violence of *Native Son.*" *Richard Wright: A Collection of Critical Essays.* Ed. Arnold Rampersad. Englewood Cliffs, NJ: Prentice, 1995. 12–25.

Budd, Louis J. *Mark Twain: The Contemporary Reviews.* Cambridge: Cambridge UP, 1999

Burgum, Edwin Berry. "The Promise of Democracy in Richard Wright's *Native Son.*" *Richard Wright's* Native Son: *A Critical Handbook.* Ed. Richard Abcarian. Belmont, CA: Wadsworth, 1970. 111–22.

Burton, Angela. (1998). "Signifyin(g) Abjection: Narrative Strategies in Toni Morrison's *Jazz.*" *Toni Morrison.* Ed. Linden Peach. New York: St. Martin's. 170–93.

Butler, Robert. *Native Son: The Emergence of a New Black Hero.* Boston: Twayne, 1991.

Carmean, Karen. *Toni Morrison's World of Fiction.* Troy, NY: Whitston, 1993.

Castiglia, Chrisopher, and Castronovo, Russ, eds. "Aesthetics and the Ends of Cultural Studies." *American Literature*, 76, 3 (September 2004).

Cawelti, John C. *Adventure, Mystery, and Romance: Formula Stories as Art and Popular Culture.* Chicago: U of Chicago P, 1976.

Caygill, Howard. *The Art of Judgment.* London: Basil Blackwell, 1989.

Chadwick-Joshua, Jocelyn. *The Jim Dilemma: Reading Race in* Huckleberry Finn. Jackson: UP of Mississippi, 1998.

Chandler, Raymond. *Farewell, My Lovely.* 1940. New York: Vintage Books, 1976.

———. *The Big Sleep.* 1939. New York: Vintage Books, 1992.

Chartier, Roger. *The Order of Books: Readers, Authors, and Libraries in Europe between the Fourteenth and Eighteenth Centuries.* Trans. Lydia G. Cochrane. Cambridge; Polity, 1992.

Chase, Richard. *The American Novel and Its Tradition.* Garden City, NY: Doubleday Anchor, 1957.

Christian, Barbara. "Layered Rhythms: Virginia Woolf and Toni Morrison." *Toni Morrison: Critical and Theoretical Approaches.* Ed. Nancy J. Peterson. Baltimore: Johns Hopkins UP, 1997. 19–36.

———. "The Race for Theory." *Cultural Critique* 6 (Spring 1987): 51–64.

Clark, Michael P. "Introduction." *Revenge of the Aesthetic: The Place of Literature in Theory Today.* Ed. Michael Clark. London: U of California P, 2000.

Clemen, Wolfgang H. "From The Development of Shakespeare's Imagery." *The Tragedy of Hamlet Prince of Denmark*. Ed. Edward Hubler. 2nd ed. New York: New American Library, 1987: 221–34.

Coleridge, Samuel Taylor. *Samuel Taylor Coleridge*. Ed. H. J. Jackson. Oxford: Oxford UP, 1985.

Collini, Stephan. "Introduction." *The Two Cultures*. Cambridge: Cambridge UP, 1998.

Collins, Jim. *Uncommon Cultures: Popular Culture and Post-modernism*. New York: Routledge, 1989.

Compagnon, Antoine. *Le Démon de la Théorie Littérature et sense commun*. Paris: Éditions de Seuil, 1998.

Cooke, Michael G. *Afro-American Literature in the Twentieth Century: The Achievement of Intimacy*. New Haven, CT: Yale UP, 1984.

Costello, Brannon. "Richard Wright's *Lawd Today!* and the Political Uses of Modernism." *African American Review* 37.1 (2003): 39–52.

Cox, James M. "A Hard Book to Take." *The Critical Response to Mark Twain's* Huckleberry Finn. Ed. Laurie Champion. New York: Greenwood Press, 1991. 171–86.

Crews, Frederick. *The Critics Bear It Away: American Fiction and the Academy* New York: Random House, 1992.

Cruz, Jon, and Justin Lewis, eds. *Viewing, Reading, Listening: Audience and Cultural Reception*. Boulder: Westview, 1994.

Dallmayr, Fred. "Adorno and Heidegger." *Diacritics*, 19.3–4 (Fall–Winter 1989): 82–100.

Dasenbrock, Reed Way. *Truth and Consequences: Intentions, Conventions, and the New Thematics*. University Park: Penn State UP, 2001.

Davidson, Cathy N., and Goldberg, David Theo. "Engaging the Humanities." *Profession 2004*. New York: Modern Language Association of America, 2004. 42–62.

DeCoste, Damon Marcel."To Blot It All Out: The Politics of Realism in Richard Wright's *Native Son*." *Style* 32 (1998): 127–147.

deFord, Miriam Allen. "Shelley, Mary Wollstonecraft Godwin." *British Authors of the Nineteenth Century*. Ed. Stanley Jasspon Kunitz and Howard Kunitz. New York: H. W. Wilson, 1936. 555–56.

Delbanco, Andrew. *Required Reading: Why Our American Classics Matter Now*. New York: Noonday, 1997.

Deleuze, Gilles. *Foucault*. Paris: Les Éditions de Minuit, 1986.

Denard, Carolyn. "The Convergence of Feminism and Ethnicity in the Fiction of Toni Morrison." *Critical Essays on Toni Morrison*. Ed. Nellie Y. McKay. Boston: G. K. Hall, 1988. 171–78.

———. "The Long, High Gaze: The Mythical Consciousness of Toni Morrison and William Faulkner." *Unflinching Gaze: Morrison and Faulkner Re-Envisioned*. Ed. Carol A. Kolmerten et al. Jackson: UP of Mississippi, 1997. 17–30.

Derrida, Jacques. "Cogito and the History of Madness." *Writing and Difference*. Trans. Alan Bass. Chicago: U of Chicago P, 1978. 31–63.

———. "Difference." *Speech and Phenomena*. Evanston, IL: Northwestern UP, 1973. 129–60.

———. *Specters of Marx: The State of the Debt, the Work of Mourning, and the New International*. Intro. Bernd Magnus and Stephen Cullenberg. Trans. Peggy Kamuf. New York: Routledge, 1994.

———. *The Truth in Painting*. Trans. Geoff Bennington and Ian McLeod. Chicago: U of Chicago P, 1987.

———. *Writing and Difference*. Trans. by Alan Bass. Chicago: The U. of Chicago P., 1978.

DeVoto, Bernard. *Mark Twain's America*. Boston: Little, Brown, 1932.

Dickens, Charles. *Oliver Twist*. New York: Penguin, 1977.

Dickinson, Roger, Ramaswami Harindranath, and Olga Linné, eds. *Approaches to Audiences*. Boulder: Westview, 1998.

Dickstein, Morris. "The Critics Who Made Us: Lionel Trilling and the Liberal Tradition." *Lionel Trilling and the Critics: Opposing Selves*. Ed. John Rodden. Lincoln: U of Nebraska P, 1999. 377–90.

Docker, John. *Postmodernism and Popular Culture: A Cultural History*. Cambridge: Cambridge UP, 1994.

Donoghue, Denis. *The American Classics A Personal Essay*. New Haven, CT: Yale UP, 2005.

———. *The Practice of Reading*. New Haven, CT: Yale UP, 1998.

Douglass, Ann. *The Feminization of American Culture*. New York: Alfred A. Knopf, 1977.

Dreiser, Theodore. *An American Tragedy*. New York: Dell, 1960.

Duckworth, Alistair, M. *The Improvement of the Estate: A Study of Jane Austen's Novels*. Baltimore: Johns Hopkins UP, 1971.

Duncan, Aswell. "The Puzzling Design of *Absalom, Absalom!*" *William Faulkner's* Absalom, Absalom!: *A Critical Casebook*. Ed. Elisabeth Muhlenfeld. New York: Garland, 1984. 93–108.

Duvall, John N. "Toni Morrison and the Anxiety of Faulknerian Influence." *Unflinching Gaze: Morrison and Faulkner Re-Envisioned*. Ed. Carol A. Kolmerten et al. Jackson: UP of Mississippi, 1997. 3–16.

———. *The Identifying Fictions of Toni Morrison: Modernist Authenticity and Postmodern Blackness*. New York: Palgrave, 2000.

Eagleton, Terry. *The Function of Criticism: From* The Spectator *to Post-Structuralism*. London: Verso, 1984.

————. *The Ideology of the Aesthetic*. Cambridge, MA: Basil Blackwell, Inc., 1990.

Easthope, Anthony. *Literary into Cultural Studies*. London: Routledge, 1991.

Ebert, Teresa. "Detecting the Phallus: Authority, Ideology, and the Production of Patriarchal Agents in Detective Fiction." *Rethinking Marxism* 5.3 (Fall 1992): 6–28.

Elden, Stuart. *Mapping the Present: Heidegger, Foucault and the Project of a Spatial History*. London: Continuum Press, 2001.

Eliot, T.S. "The Boy and the River: Without Beginning or End." *The Critical Response to Mark Twain's* Huckleberry Finn. Ed. Laurie Champion. Westport, CT: Greenwood Press, 1991. 44–49.

Elliott, Emory. "Introduction." *Aesthetics in a Multicultural Age*. Ed. Emory Elliott, Louis Freitas, and Jeffrey Rhyne. New York: Oxford UP, 2002.

Emerson, O. B. *Faulkner's Early Reputation in America*. Ann Arbor: UMI Research Press, 1984.

Empson, William. "Updating Revenge Tragedy." Rpt in *Hamlet*. Ed. Cyrus Hoy. 2nd ed. New York: W.W. Norton & Co., 1992: 283–94.

Fabre, Michel. "Beyond Naturalism?" *Richard Wright*. Ed. Harold Bloom. New York: Chelsea House, 1987. 37–56.

————. *Richard Wright: Books and Writers*. Jackson: UP of Mississippi, 1990.

Faulkner, William. *Absalom, Absalom!* New York: Random House, 1964.

————. *Light in August*. 1959. New York: Random House, 1990.

Feenberg, Andrew. *Lukács, Marx and the Sources of Critical Theory*. Totowa, NJ: Rowman and Littlefield, 1981.

Fergus, Jan. *Jane Austen and the Didactic Novel*. Totowa, NJ: Barnes & Noble, 1983. 11–37.

Fergusson, Margaret. W. "*Hamlet*: letters and spirits." Rpt. in *Hamlet*. 2nd ed. Ed. by Cyrus Hoy. New York: W.W. Norton & Co., 1992: 246–62

Ferris, Ina. *The Achievement of Literary Authority: Gender, History, and the Waverly Novels*. Ithaca, NY: Cornell UP, 1991.

Fish, Stanley. "Being Interdisciplinary Is So Very Hard to Do," *Profession 89*: 15–22.

————. *Is There a Text in this Class? The Authority of Interpretive Communities*. Cambridge, MA: Harvard UP, 1980.

————. "Literature in the Reader: Affective Stylistics." *From Formalism to Post-structuralism*. Ed. Jane P. Tompkins. Baltimore: John Hopkins UP, 1980. 70–100.

————. *Professional Correctness: Literary Studies and P)olitical Change*. Oxford: Clarendon Press, 1995.

Fishburn, Katherine. *Richard Wright's Hero: The Faces of a Rebel-Victim*. Metuchen, NJ: Scarecrow, 1977.

Flint, Kate. *The Woman Reader, 1837–1914*. Oxford, 1993.

Fluck, Winnifred. "Aesthetics and Cultural Studies." *Aesthetics in a Multicultural Age*. Ed. Emory Elliott, Louis Freitas, and Jeffrey Rhyne. New York: Oxford UP, 2002. 79–104.

———. "The Search for Distance: Negation and Negativity in Wolfgang Iser's Literary Theory." *New Literary History* 31, 1 (Winter 2000): 175–210.

Foley, Barbara. "Marxism in the Poststructuralist Moment: Some Notes on the Problem of Revising Marx." *Cultural Critique* 15 (1990): 5–37.

———. "The Politics of Poetics: Ideology and Narrative Form in *An American Tragedy* and *Native Son*." *Richard Wright: Critical Perspectives Past and Present*. Ed. Henry Louis Gates, Jr., and K. A. Appiah. New York: Amistad, 1993. 188–99.

Forry, Steven Earl. *Hideous Progenies: Dramatizations of* Frankenstein *from Mary Shelley to the Present*. Philadelphia: U of Pennsylvania P, 1990.

Foster, Thomas. *How to Read Literature Like a Professor: A Lively and Entertaining Guide to Reading Between the Lines*. New York: Harper, 2003.

Foucault, Michel. *History of Sexuality, Vol. 1: An Introduction*. Trans. Robert Hurley. New York: Vintage, 1980.

———. "My Body, This Paper, This Fire." *Aesthetics, Method, and Epistemology*. Ed. James D. Fabion. Trans. Robert Hurley et al. New York: The New Press, 1998. 394–417.

———. *The Order of Things: An Archaeology of the Human Sciences*. Trans. Alan Sheridan. New York: Pantheon, 1970.

Fox-Genovese, Elizabeth. "Unspeakable Things Unspoken: Ghosts and Memories in the Narratives of African-American Women." *Toni Morrison's Beloved*. Ed. Harold Bloom. Philadelphia: Chelsea House, 1999. 97–114.

Frow, John. *Cultural Studies and Cultural Value*. Oxford: Clarendon Press, 1995.

———. "Literature as Regime (Meditations on an Emergence)." *The Question of Literature: The Place of the Literary in Contemporary Theory*. Ed. Elizabeth Beaumont Bissell. Manchester: Manchester UP, 2002. 142–55.

———. *Marxism and Literary History*. Cambridge, MA: Harvard University Press, 1986.

———. "On Literature and Cultural Studies." *The Aesthetics of Cultural Studies*. Ed. Michael Bérubé. Oxford: Blackwell, 2005. 44–57.

———. *Time and Commodity Culture*. Oxford: Clarendon Press, 1997.

Gair, Christopher. "The American Dickens." *A Companion to Mark Twain*. Ed. Peter Messent and Louis J. Budd. Oxford: Blackwell, 2005. 141–56.

Gard, Roger. *Jane Austen's Novels: The Art of Clarity*. New Haven, CT: Yale UP, 1992.

Gardner, Joseph H. *Dickens in America: Twain, Howells, James, and Norris.* New York: Garland, 1988.

Gates, Henry Louis Jr. *Figures in Black: Words, Signs, and the "Racial" Self.* New York: Oxford UP, 1987.

———. "Harlem on Our Minds." *Critical Inquiry.* 24.1 (1997): 1–12.

Gates, Henry Louis, Jr., and K. A. Appiah, eds. *Richard Wright: Critical Perspectives Past and Present.* New York: Amistad, 1993.

———. *Zora Neale Hurston: Critical Perspectives Past and Present.* New York: Amistad, 1993.

Gayle, Addison, Jr. "Richard Wright: Beyond Nihilism." *Richard Wright's* Native Son: *A Critical Handbook.* Ed. Richard Abcarian. Belmont, CA: Wadsworth, 1970. 177–82.

George, Stephen K. "The Horror of Bigger Thomas: The Perception of Form without Face in Richard Wright's *Native Son.*" *African American Review,* 31 (1997): 497–504.

Gibson, Donald B. "Wright's Invisible Native Son." *Richard Wright: A Collection of Critical Essays.* Ed. Richard Macksey and Frank E. Moore. Englewood Cliffs, NJ: Prentice, 1984. 95–105.

Gilbert, Sandra M., and Gubar, Susan. *The Madwoman in the Attic: The Woman Writer and the Nineteenth-Century Literary Imagination.* New Haven, CT: Yale UP, 1979.

———. "Tradition and the Female Talent." *The Poetics of Gender.* Ed. Nancy K. Miller. New York: Columbia UP, 1986. 183–207.

Gilligan, Carol. *In a Different Voice.* Cambridge, MA: Harvard UP, 1982.

Glazener, Nancy. *Reading for Realism: The History of a U.S. Literary Institution, 1850–1920.* Durham, NC: Duke UP, 1997.

Gloster, Hugh M., *Negro Voices in American Fiction.* Chapel Hill: U of North Carolina P, 1948.

Goldstein, Philip. *Communities of Cultural Value: Reception Study, Political Differences, and Literary History.* Lanham, MD: Lexington, 2001.

Graff, Gerald. *Literature Against Itself: Literary Ideas in Modern Society.* Chicago: U of Chicago P, 1979.

———. *Professing Literature: An Institutional History.* Chicago: U of Chicago P, 1987.

Graff, Gerald, and Phelan, James, eds. *Adventures of Huckleberry Finn.* 2nd ed. New York: Bedford/St. Martin's, 2004.

Graham, Hugh Savis, and Diamond, Nancy. *The Rise of American Research Universities: Elites and Challengers in the Postwar Era.* Baltimore: Johns Hopkins UP 1997.

Gray, Donald J., ed. Pride and Prejudice: *An Authoritative Text, Backgrounds and Sources, Criticism.* 2nd ed. New York: W. W. Norton, 1993.

Green, Michelle. "Sara Paretsky's Cult Heroine Is a Woman's Woman—V.I. Warshawski, the Funky Feminist Private Eye." *People Weekly*, 14 May 1990: 132–3.

Greenblatt, Stephen. "Towards a Poetics of Culture," *The New Historicism*. Ed. H. Aram Veeser. New York: Routledge, 1989. 1–14.

———. "What Is the History of Literature?" *Critical Inquiry*, 23.3 (Spring 1997): 460–81.

———. *Hamlet in Purgatory*. Princeton: Princeton University Press, 2001.

Grewal, Gurleen. *Circles of Sorrow, Lines of Struggle: The Novels of Toni Morrison*. Baton Rouge: Louisiana State UP, 1998.

Grimes, William. "Learning How to Read Slowly Again." *The New York Times*. Sept 22, 2006. <http://www.nytimes.com/2006/09/22/books/22read.html>

Grossberg, Lawrence, James Hay, and Ellen Wartella, eds. *The Audience and Its Landscape*. Boulder: Westview Press, 1996.

Grylls, R. Glynn. *Mary Shelley: A Biography*. London: Oxford UP, 1938.

Guetti, James. "*Absalom, Absalom!* The Extended Metaphor." *William Faulkner's* Absalom, Absalom!*: A Critical Casebook*. Ed.Elisabeth Muhlenfeld. New York: Garland, 1984. 65–92.

Guillory, John. *Cultural Capital: The Problem of Literary Canon Formation*. Chicago: U of Chicago P, 1993.

———. "Literary Study and the Modern System of the Disciplines." *Disciplinarity at the fin de siècle*. Ed. Amanda Anderson and Joseph Valente. Princeton, NJ: Princeton UP, 2002. 19–43.

———."The Sokal Affair and the History of Criticism." *Critical Inquiry* 28 (Winter 2002): 470–508.

Gunn, Giles. "The Pragmatics of the Aesthetic." *Aesthetics in a Multicultural Age*. Edited by Emory Elliott, Louis Freitas, and Jeffrey Rhyne. New York: Oxford University Press, 2002: 61–77.

Gwin, Minrose. C. *The Feminine and Faulkner: Reading (Beyond) Sexual Difference*. Knoxville: U of Tennessee P, 1990.

Habermas, Jürgen. *The Theory of Communicative Action*. Vol.1. Trans. by Thomas McCarthy. Boston: Beacon Press, 1981.

Hakutani, Yoshinobu. *Richard Wright and Racial Discourse*. Columbia: U of Missouri P, 1996.

Hammond, Ray. *The Modern Frankenstein: Fiction Becomes Fact*. New York: Blandford, 1986.

Handley, Graham. *Jane Austen*. New York: St. Martin's, 1992.

Harding, D. W. *Regulated Hatred and other essays on Jane Austen*. London: Athlone Press, 1998.

Hardy, Thomas. *Tess of the D'Urbervilles*. Ed. William E. Buckler. Boston: Houghton Mifflin, 1960.

Hawkes, Terence. "Telmah." *Shakespeare and the Question of Theory*. Ed. by Patricia Parker and Geoffrey Hartmann. New York: Methuen, 1985: 310–32.

Heidegger, Martin. *Being and Time*. Trans. John Macquarrie and Edward Robinson. 1926. New York: Harper & Row, 1962.

———. *Poetry, Language, and Thought*. Trans. Albert Hofstadter. New York: Harper & Row, 1975.

———. "The Question of Technology." *Martin Heidegger Basic Writings from Being and Time (1927) to The Task of Thinking (1964)*. Ed. David Farrell Krell. 2nd rev. and expanded ed. New York: HarperCollins, 1993. 307–42.

Heinz, Denise. *The Dilemma of "Double-Consciousness": Toni Morrison's Novels*. Athens: U of Georgia P, 1993.

Hermes, Joke. "Cultural Citizenship and Crime Fiction: Politics and Interpretive Community." *European Journal of Cultural Studies* 3.2 (May 2000): 215–32.

Hirsch, E. D. Jr. *Cultural Literacy: What Every American Needs to Know*. New York: Vintage Books, 1988.

———. *Validity in Interpretation*. New Haven, CT: Yale UP, 1967.

Hoeveler, Diane. "Vindicating *Northanger Abbey*: Mary Wollstonecraft, Jane Austen, and Gothic Feminism." *Jane Austen and Discourses of Feminism*. Ed. Devoney Looser. New York: St. Martin's, 1995. 117–36.

Hogan, Michael. "Built on the Ashes: The Fall of the House of Sutpen and the Rise of the House of Sethe." *Unflinching Gaze: Morrison and Faulkner Re-Envisioned*. Ed. Carol A. Kolmerten et al. Jackson: UP of Mississippi, 1997. 167–81.

Holland, Norman. "Unity Identity Text Self." *Reader-Response Criticism: From Formalism to Post-Structuralism*. Ed. Jane P. Tompkins. Baltimore: Johns Hopkins UP, 1980. 201–32.

Howe, Irving. "Black Boys and Native Sons." *Richard Wright's* Native Son: *A Critical Handbook*. Ed. Richard Abcarian. Belmont, CA: Wadsworth, 1970. 135–43.

———. *William Faulkner: A Critical Study*. New York: Vintage, 1962.

Howells, William Dean. "Mark Twain: An Inquiry." In *Huck Finn among the Critics: A Centennial Selection*. Ed. M. Thomas Inge. Frederick, MD: University Publications of America, 1985. 53–66.

Hoy, David Cousins. *The Critical Circle: Literature, History, and Philosophical Hermeneutics*. Berkeley: University of California Press, 1982.

Hunter, Paul J. ed. *Mary Shelley*, Frankenstein: *contexts, nineteenth-century responses, criticism*. New York: W. W. Norton, 1996.

Hurston, Zora Neale. "How It Feels to be Colored Me," *I Love Myself When I am Laughing . . . And Then Again When I Am Looking Mean and*

Impressive: A Zora Neale Hurston Reader. Ed. Alice Walker. Intro. Mary Helen Washington. New York: Feminist P, 1979. 152–55.

———. *Their Eyes Were Watching God.* New York: Harper & Row, 1990.

Huyssen, Andreas. "Mapping the Postmodern." *New German Critique* 33 (1984): 5–52.

Hynes, Joseph. "*Native Son* Fifty Years Later." *Cimarron Review* 102 (1993): 91–7.

Irwin, John T. "The Dead Father in Faulkner." *The Fictional Father: Lacanian Readings of the Text.* Ed. Robert Con Davis. Amherst: U of Massachusetts P, 1981. 147–68.

Iser, Wolfgang. *The Act of Reading: A Theory of Aesthetic Response.* Baltimore: Johns Hopkins UP, 1972.

———. *The Fictive and the Imaginary: Charting Literary Anthropology.* Baltimore: John Hopkins University Press, 1993.

———. *The Range of Interpretation.* New York: Columbia University Press, 2000.

Jackson. Esther Merle. "The American Negro and the Image of the Absurd." *Richard Wright: A Collection of Critical Essays.* Ed. Richard Macksey and Frank E. Moore. Englewood Cliffs, NJ: Prentice, 1984. 129–38.

Jameson, Fredric. "How Not to Historicize Theory." *Critical Inquiry.* 34, 3 (2008): 563–82.

———. *Late Marxism: Adorno, or the Persistence of the Dialectic.* New York: Verso, 1990.

———. *The Political Unconscious: Narrative as a Socially Symbolic Act.* Ithaca, NY: Cornell UP, 1981.

Jancovich, Mark. *The Cultural Politics of the New Criticism.* Cambridge: Cambridge UP, 1993.

JanMohamed, Abdul R., *The Death-Bound-Subject: Richard Wright's Archaeology of Death.* Durham, NC: Duke, 2005.

Jauss, Hans Robert. *Toward an Aesthetic of Reception.* Trans. Timothy Bahti. Minneapolis: U of Minnesota P, 1982.

———. *Aesthetic Experience and Literary Hermeneutics.* Trans. Michael Shaw. Intro. Wlad Godzich. Minneapolis: University of Minnesota Press, 1982.

Jehlen, Myra. *Class and Character in Faulkner's South.* New York: Columbia UP, 1976.

Jenkins, Henry. *Textual Poachers: Television Fans and Participatory Culture.* New York: Routledge, 1992.

Jones, Darryl. *Horror: A Thematic History in Fiction and Film.* London: Arnold, 2002.

Jordan, June. "On Richard Wright and Zora Neale Hurston: Notes Toward a Balancing of Love and Hatred." *Black World* (August 1974): 4–8.

Joughin, John J., and Simon Malpas, eds. *The New Aestheticism*. Manchester: Manchester UP, 2003.

————. "Introduction." *The New Aestheticism*. Ed. John J. Joughin and Simon Malpas. Manchester: Manchester UP, 2003. 1–22.

Joyce, Joyce Ann. "Black Woman Scholar, Critic, and Teacher: The Inextricable Relationship between Race, Sex, and Class." *NLH* 22 (1991): 543–65.

————. *Richard Wright's Art of Tragedy*. Iowa City: U of Iowa P, 1986.

Jumonville, Neil. *Critical Crossings: The New York Intellectuals in Postwar America*. Berkeley: U of California P, 1991.

Karaganis, Joseph. "Naturalism's Nation: Toward *An American Tragedy*." *American Literature*, 72: 153–80.

Kazin, Alfred. "The Stillness of *Light in August*." *William Faulkner: Three Decades of Criticism*. Ed. and intro. Frederick J. Hoffman and Olga. W. Vickery. New York: Harcourt Brace Jovanovich, 1960. 247–78.

Kelley, Robin D. G. *Race Rebels: Culture, Politics, and the Black Working Class*. New York: Free P, 1994.

Kelly, Michael. *Iconoclasm in Aesthetics*. Cambridge: Cambridge UP, 2003.

Kennedy, James G. "The Form and Content of *Native Son*." *College English* 34 (1972): 269–83.

Kermode, Frank. *Pleasure and Change: The Aesthetics of Canon*. Ed. and Intro. Robert Alter. Oxford: Oxford University Press, 2004.

Kernan, Alvin. *Samuel Johnson and the Impact of Print*. Princeton, NJ: Princeton UP, 1989.

————. *The Death of Literature*. New Haven, CT: Yale UP, 1990.

Kirkham, Margaret. "Postscript: Jane Austen and the Critical Tradition." *Jane Austen: Critical Assessments*. Ed. Ian Littlewood. East Sussex: Helm Information Ltd, 1998. 1:246–59.

Klancher, Jon. *The Making of English Reading Audiences, 1790–1832*. Madison: U of Wisconsin P, 1987.

Knight, G. Wilson. *The Wheel of Fire: Essays in Interpretation of Shakespeare's Somber Tragedies*. London: Oxford University Press, 1930.

Koch, John. "Sara Paretsky Lets the Private Eye She Created Do the Talking." *The Boston Globe*, 5 February 1992: 35.

Kodat, Catherine Gunther. "A Postmodern *Absalom, Absalom!*, a Modern *Beloved*: The Dialectic of Form." *Unflinching Gaze: Morrison and Faulkner Re-Envisioned*. Ed. Carol A. Kolmerten et al. Jackson: UP of Mississippi, 1997. 181–98.

Kolmerton, Carol A., et al. "Introduction." *Unflinching Gaze: Morrison and Faulkner Re-Envisioned*. Ed. Carol A. Kolmerten et al. Jackson: UP of Mississippi, 1997. ix–xv.

Krauth, Leland. *Mark Twain and Company: Six Literary Relations.* Athens: University of Georgia Press, 2003.

Kreiger, Murray. "The 'Imaginary' and Its Enemies." *New Literary History* 31:1 (Winter 2000): 130–74.

Krumholz, Linda. "The Ghosts of Slavery: Historical Recovery in Toni Morrison's *Beloved.*" *Toni Morrison's* Beloved. Ed. Harold Bloom. Philadelphia: Chelsea House, 1999. 79–95.

Kuyk, Dirk, Jr. *Sutpen's Design: Interpreting Faulkner's* Absalom: UP of Virginia, 1990.

Langford, Gerald. *Faulkner's Revision of* Absalom, Absalom!: *A Collation of the Manuscript and the Published Book.* Austin: U of Texas P, 1971.

Lascelles, Mary. "From *Jane Austen and Her Art.*" Cited in *Jane Austen*: Northanger Abbey *and* Persuasion *A Casebook.* Ed. B. C. Southam. London: MacMillan, 1976. 62–68.

Lauter, Paul. *From Walden Pond to Jurassic Park: Activism, Culture, & American Studies.* Durham, NC: Duke UP, 2001.

Lawrence, David. "Fleshly Ghosts and Ghostly Flesh: The Word and the Body in *Beloved.*" *Toni Morrison's* Beloved. Ed. Harold Bloom. Philadelphia: Chelsea House, 1999. 45–56.

Lee, Robert A. "Inside Narratives." *Richard Wright.* Edited by Harold Bloom. New York: Chelsea House, 1987: 109–26.

Leitch, Vincent B. *American Literary Criticism from the Thirties to the Eighties.* New York: Columbia UP, 1988.

Lentricchia, Frank, and DuBois, Andrew, eds. *Close Reading: The Reader.* Durham: Duke University Press, 2003.

Levin, Harry. *The Question of* Hamlet. New York: Oxford University Press, 1959.

Levine, George. "*Frankenstein* and the Tradition of Realism." *Frankenstein.* Mary Shelley. Ed. J. Paul Hunter. New York: W. W. Norton, 1996. 208–13.

Levine, George, and U. C. Knoepflmacher. "Preface." *The Endurance of* Frankenstein: *Essays on Mary Shelley's Novel.* Ed. George Levine and U. C. Knoepflmacher. Berkeley: U of California P, 1979.

Levine, George, and Owen Thomas, eds. *The Scientist vs. the Humanist.* New York: W.W. Norton, 1963

Lewes, G. H. "Recent Novels: French and English." Cited in Graham Handley, *Jane Austen* New York: St. Martin's, 1992. 16–17.

Lind, Ise Dusoir. "The Design and Meaning of *Absalom, Absalom!*" *William Faulkner: Three Decades of Criticism.* Ed. Frederick J. Hoffman and Olga W. Vickery. New York: Harcourt, Brace, Jovanovich, 1960. 278–304.

Lipking, Lawrence. "*Frankenstein,* the True Story; or, Rousseau Judges Jean-Jacques." *Frankenstein.* Mary Shelley. Ed. J. Paul Hunter. New York: W. W. Norton, 1996. 313–332.

Loesberg, Jonathan. *A Return to Aesthetics*. Standord: Stanford University Press, 2005.

London Morning Post July 30, 1823. Cited in *Frankenstein; or the Modern Prometheus*. Ed. Susan J. Wolfson. New York: Longman, 2003. 327.

Longhurst, Derek. "Sherlock Holmes: Adventures of an English Gentleman 1887–1894." *Gender, Genre and Narrative Pleasure*. Edited by Derek Longhurst. London: Unwin Hyman, 1989: 51–66.

MacCarthy, B. G. *The Later Women Novelists: 1744–1818*. Oxford: Blackwell, 1947.

Macherey, Pierre. *Histoires de dinosuare Faire de la Philosophie 1965–1997*. Paris: Presse Universitaires de France, 1999.

———. *In a Materialist Way: Selected Essays by Pierre Macherey*. Ed. Warren Montag. Trans. Ted Stolze. London: Verso, 1998.

———. *The Object of Literature*. Trans. David Macey. Cambridge: Cambridge UP, 1995.

Mailloux, Steven. *Reception Histories: Rhetoric, Pragmatism, and American Cultural Politics*. Ithaca: Cornell UP, 1998.

———. *Rhetorical Power*. Ithaca, NY: Cornell UP, 1989.

Marcus, Stephen. "*Frankenstein*: Myths of Scientific and Medical Knowledge and Stories of Human Relations." *The Southern Review*. 38:1 (Winter 2002): 188–201.

Margolies, Edward. *Native Sons: A Critical Study of Twentieth-Century Negro American Authors*. Philadelphia: Lippincott, 1968.

Marx, Leo. "Mr. Eliot, Mr. Trilling, and *Huckleberry Finn*." *The Critical Response to Mark Twain's* Huckleberry Finn. Ed. Laurie Champion. Westport: Greenwood, 1991. 50–60.

Matus, Jill. *Toni Morrison*. Manchester: Manchester UP, 1998.

Maxwell, William J. *New Negro, Old Left: African American Writing and Communism between the Wars*. New York: Columbia UP, 1999.

Mbalia, Doreathea Drummond. *Toni Morrison's Developing Class Consciousness*. 2nd ed. Selingsgrove: Susquehanna UP, 2004.

McKay, Nellie Y. Introduction. *Toni Morrison's* Beloved: *A Casebook*. Ed. William L. Andrews and Nellie Y. McKay. New York: Oxford UP, 1999. 3–19.

McKee, Patricia. *Producing American Races: Henry James, William Faulkner, Toni Morrison* Durham, NC: Duke UP, 1999.

McNay, Lois. *Foucault and Feminism*. Boston: Northeastern UP, 1993.

Mellor, Anne K. *Mary Shelley, Her Life, Her Fiction, Her Monsters*. New York: Routledge, 1988.

———. "Possessing Nature: The Female in *Frankenstein*." *Frankenstein*. Mary Shelley. Ed. J. Paul Hunter. New York: W. W. Norton, 1996. 274–86.

Menegaldo, Gilles. "Introduction." *Autour de Frankenstein (Lectures critiques)*. Ed. Gilles Menegaldo. Poitier: Cahiers Forell, 1999.

Menken, H. L. "The Burden of Humor." *Huck Finn among the Critics: A Centennial Selection*. Ed. M. Thomas Inge. Frederick, MD: University Publications of America, 1985. 67–71.

Messer-Davidow, Ellen. *Disciplining Feminism: From Social Activism to Academic Discourse*. Durham, NC: Duke UP, 2002.

Michaels, Walter Benn. *Our America: Nativism, Modernism, and Pluralism*. Durham, NC: Duke UP, 1995.

————. *The Shape of the Signifier: 1967 to the End of History*. Princeton, NJ: Princeton UP, 2004.

Miller, Paul Allen. "The Art of Self-Fashioning, or Foucault on Plato and Derrida." *Foucault Studies* 2 (May 2005): 54–74.

Miller, Thomas P. *The Formation of College English: Rhetoric and Belles Lettres in the British Cultural Provinces*. Pittsburgh: U of Pittsburgh P, 1997.

Millgate, Michael. (1987). "'A Novel: Not an Anecdote': Faulkner's *Light in August*." *New Essays on* Light on August. Ed.Michael Millgate. Cambridge: Cambridge UP: 31–54.

Mobley, Marilyn Saunders. "A Different Remembering: Memory, History, and Meaning in Toni Morrison's *Beloved*." *Toni Morrison's* Beloved. Ed. Harold Bloom. Philadelphia: Chelsea House, 1999. 189–99.

Moers, Ellen. "Female Gothic: The Monster's Mother." *Frankenstein*. Mary Shelley. Ed. J. Paul Hunter. New York: W. W. Norton, 1996. 214–224.

Moler, Kenneth. L. *Jane Austen's Art of Allusion*. Lincoln: U of Nebraska P, 1968.

Montag, Warren. *Louis Althusser*. New York: Palgrave MacMillan, 2003.

Montauzon, Christine de. *Faulkner's* Absalom, Absalom! *and Interpretability: The Inexplicable Unseen*. New York: Peter Lang, 1985.

Morgan, Susan J. *In the Meantime: Character and Perception in Jane Austen's Fiction*. Cited in *Jane Austen: Critical Asssments*. Ed. Ian Smallwood. East Sussex: Helm Information, 1998. 3:186–92.

Morrison, Toni. *Beloved*. New York: Plume, 1988.

————. *The Bluest Eye*. 1970
New York, Plume, 1994.

————. *Jazz*. New York: Plume, 1992.

Morton, Timothy, ed. *A Routledge Literary Sourcebook on Mary Shelley's* Frankenstein. New York: Routledge, 2002.

Mudrick, Marvin. *Jane Austen: Irony as Defense and Discovery*. Princeton, NJ: Princeton UP, 1952.

Neil, Edward. The Politics of Jane Austen. New York: St. Martin's, 1999.

Newman, Gerald. *The Rise of English Nationalism: A Cultural History, 1740–1830*. New York: St. Martin's, 1987.

Nilon, Charles H. "The Ending of *Huckleberry Finn*: 'Freeing the Free Negro.'" *Satire or Evasion? Black Perspectives on* Huckleberry Finn. Ed.

James S. Leonard, Thomas A. Tenney, and Thadious M. Davis. Durham, NC: Duke UP, 1992. 62–76.

Nissen, Axel. *Bret Harte: Prince and Pauper*. Jackson: UP of Mississippi, 2000.

Norris, Christopher. "Language, Truth and Ideology: Orwell and the Post-War Left." *Inside the Myth: Orwell: Views from the Left*. London: Lawrence and Wishart, 1984. 242–62.

———. "What is Enlightenment? Kant According to Foucault." *Reconstructing Foucault: Essays in the Wake of the 80s*. Ed. Silvia Caporate-Bizzini and Richardo Miguel-Alfonso. Amsterdam: Editions Rodopi, 1994. 53–138.

Novak, Phillip. "Signifying Silences: Morrison's Soundings in the Faulknerian Void." *Unflinching Gaze: Morrison and Faulkner Re-Envisioned*. Ed.Carol A. Kolmerten et al. Jackson: UP of Mississippi, 1997. 199–216.

O'Donnell, George Marion. "Faulkner's Mythology." *William Faulkner: Three Decades of Criticism*. Ed. Frederick J. Hoffman and Olga W. Vickery. New York: Harcourt, Brace, Jovanovich, 1960: 82–93.

Ohmanns, Richard. *English in America: A Radical View of the Profession*. New York: Oxford UP, 1976.

———. *Politics of Knowledge: The Commercialization of the University, the Professions, and Print Culture*. Middletown, CT: Wesleyan UP, 2003.

Osborne, Peter. "A Marxism for the Postmodern: Jameson's Adorno." *New German Critique*, 56 (Spring-Summer 1992): 171–92

Paine, Albert. *Mark Twain, a Biography; The Personal and Literary Life of Samuel Langhorne Clemens*. New York, London, Harper & Brothers, 1912.

Panek, LeRoy Lad. *New Hard-Boiled Writers 1970s-1990s*. Bowling Green: Bowling Green State U Popular P, 2000. 67–84.

Paretsky, Sara. *Bitter Medicine*. New York: Ballantine, 1987.

———. *Blacklist*. New York: Signet, 2003.

———. *Blood Shot*. New York: Dell, 1988.

———. *Burn Marks*. New York: Dell, 1990.

———. *Deadlock*. New York: Ballantine, 1984.

———. *Indemnity Only*. New York: Dell, 1992.

———. *Killing Orders*. New York: Ballantine, 1985.

Parker, Robert Dale. Absalom, Absalom!: *The Questioning of Fictions*. New York: Twayne, 1991.

Parrinder, Patrick. *Authors and Authority: A Study of English Literary Criticism and its Relation to Culture, 1750–1900*. London: Routledge & Kegan Paul, 1977.

Peach, Linden. *Toni Morrison*. New York: St. Martin's, 2000.

Pearson, Jacqueline. *Women's Reading in Britain, 1750–1835: A Dangerous Recreation*. Cambridge; New York: Cambridge UP, 1999.

Pensky, Max. "Editor's Introduction: Adorno's Actuality." *The Actuality of Adorno: Critical Essays on Adorno and the Postmodern.* Ed. Max Pensky. Albany: SUNY Press, 1997. 1–21.

Peterson, Nancy J. "Introduction." *Toni Morrison: Critical and Theoretical Approaches.* Ed. Nancy J. Peterson. Baltimore: Johns Hopkins UP, 1997. 1–15.

Pietz, William. "The PostColonialism of Cold War Discourse." *Social Text* 19–20 (1988): 56–76.

Pinkney, Edward Coote. "The New Frankenstein." *The Life and Works of Edward Coote Pinkney.* Ed. Thomas Ollive Mabbott and Frank Lester Pleadwell. New York: Macmillan, 1926. 192–97.

Pitavy, François L. *Faulkner's* Light in August. Bloomington: Indiana UP, 1973.

Pizer, Donald. "Late Nineteenth-Century Realism: An Essay in Definition." *Nineteenth-Century Fiction,* 16.3 (1961): 263–69.

———. *The Theory and Practice of American Literary Naturalism: Selected Essays and Reviews.* Carbondale: Southern Illinois UP, 1993.

Plain, Gill. *Twentieth-Century Crime Fiction*: *Gender, Sexuality, and the Body.* Edinburgh: Edinburgh UP, 2001.

Plasa, Carl. *Toni Morrison* Beloved. New York: Columbia UP, 1998.

Poirier, Richard. "Strange Gods in Jefferson, Mississippi: Analysis of *Absalom, Absalom!" Twentieth Century Interpretations of* Absalom, Absalom! Ed. Arnold Goldman. Englewood Cliffs, NJ: Prentice-Hall, 1971. 12–31.

Poovey, Mary. "'My Hideous Progeny': The Lady and the Monster." *Mary Shelley,* Frankenstein: *contexts, nineteenth-century responses, criticism.* Ed. J. Paul Hunter. New York: W. W. Norton, 1996. 251–61.

Pope, Rebecca. "'Friends Is a Weak Word for It': Female Friendship and the Spectre of Lesbianism in Sara Paretsky." *Feminism in Women's Detective Fiction.* Ed. Glenwood Irons. Toronto: Toronto UP, 1995. 157–70.

Portelli, Alessandro. "Everybody's Healing Novel: *Native Son* and Its Contemporary Critical Context." *Mississippi Quarterly: The Journal of Southern Cultures* 50 (1997): 255–265.

Porter, Carolyn. "*Absalom, Absalom!* (Un)Making the Father." *The Cambridge Companion to William Faulkner.* Ed. Philip M. Weinstein. Cambridge: Cambridge UP, 1995. 168–96.

Radway, Janice A. *A Feeling for Books: The Book-of-the Month Club, Literary Taste, and Middle-Class Desire.* Chapel Hill: U of North Carolina P, 1997.

———. *Reading the Romance: Women, Patriarchy, and Popular Literature.* Chapel Hill: U of North Caroline P, 1984.

———. "What's the Matter with Reception Studies?: Some Thoughts on the Disciplinary Origins, Conceptual Constraints, and Persistent Viability of a Paradigm." *New Directions in American Reception Study.* Ed. Philip Goldstein and James L. Machor. New York: Oxford University Press, 2008: 508–48.

Railey, Kevin. *Natural Aristocracy: History, Ideology, and the Production of William Faulkner.* Tuscaloosa: U of Alabama P, 1999.

Rancière, Jacques. *La Parole Muette.* Paris: Hachette Littératures, 1998.

———. *Le partage du sensible: esthetique et politique.* Paris: La Fabrique-éditions, 1998.

———. *The Politics of Aesthetics: The Distribution of the Sensible.* New York: Continuum, 2004.

———. "The Sublime from Lyotard to Schiller: Two Readings of Kant and Their Political Significance." *Radical Philosophy,* 126 (July/August 2004): 8–15.

Rawson, Claude. Review of *Bride of Frankenstein: A New Biography of the Woman Who Was at the Center of the Romantic Movement but Is Remembered for a Horror Story. New York Times Book Review,* 7 Oct 2001, v106, 11(1).

Readings, Bill. "The University without Culture?" *New Literary History,* xxvi, 3 (Summer 1995): 465–92.

Reilly, John M. "Giving Bigger a Voice." *Twentieth Century Interpretations of* Native Son*: A Collection of Critical Essays.* Ed. Houston Baker. Englewood Cliffs: Prentice, 1972. 35–62.

Reilly, John M. ed. *Richard Wright: The Critical Reception.* New York: Franklin, 1978.

Richter, David, ed. *The Critical Tradition: Classic Texts and Contemporary Trends.* Boston: Bedford, 1998.

Riquelme, John Paul. "Introduction: Wolfgang Iser's Aesthetic Politics: Reading as Fieldwork." *New Literary History* 31, 1 (Winter 2000): 7–12.

Roberts, David. "Art and Myth: Adorno and Heidegger." *Thesis Eleven* 58 (August 1999): 19–34.

Robinson, Charles. *The Frankenstein Notebooks.* New York: Garland, 1996.

Robinson, Forrest G. "The Characterization of Jim in *Huckleberry Finn.*" *The Critical Response to Mark Twain's* Huckleberry Finn. Ed. Laurie Champion. New York: Greenwood, 1991. 207–25.

Rodrigues, Eusebio L. "Experiencing *Jazz.*" *Toni Morrison.* Ed. Linden Peach. New York: St. Martin's, 1998. 154–69.

Rody, Caroline. "'History,' 'Rememory,' and a 'Clamor for a Kiss.'" *Toni Morrison's* Beloved. Ed. Harold Bloom. Philadelphia: Chelsea House, 1999. 155–75.

Rorty, Richard. *Achieving Our Country: Leftist Thought in Twentieth-Century America.* Cambridge, MA: Harvard UP, 1998.

———. *Essays on Heidegger and Others.* Cambridge: Cambridge UP, 1991.

Rose, Ellen Cronan. "Custody Battles: Reproducing Knowledge about *Frankenstein*." *NLH* 26.4 (Autumn 1995): 809–32.

Ross, Andrew. *No Respect: Intellectuals and Popular Culture*. New York: Routledge, 1989.

Ross, Trevor. *The Making of the English Literary Canon: From the Middle Ages to the Late Eighteenth Century*. Montreal: McGill-Queen's UP, 1998.

Rowley, Hazel. *Richard Wright: The Life and Times*. New York: Holt, 2001.

Rubenstein, Roberta. "History and Story, Sign and Design: Faulknerian and Postmodern Voices in *Jazz*." In *Unflinching Gaze: Morrison and Faulkner Re-Envisioned*. Ed. Carol A. Kolmerten et al. Jackson: UP of Mississippi, 1997: 152–64.

Rudolph, John L. *Scientists in the Classroom: The Cold War Reconstruction of American Science Education*. New York: Palgrave, 2002.

Rushdy, Ashraf H. A., "Daughters Signifyin(g) History: The Example of Toni Morrison's *Beloved*." *Toni Morrison*. Ed. Linden Peach. New York: St. Martin's, 1998. 140–53.

Said, Edward. *The World, the Text, and the Critic*. Cambridge, MA: Harvard UP, 1983.

Sawicki, Jana. *Disciplining Foucault: Feminism, Power, and the Body*. New York: Routledge, 1991.

Schaub, Thomas. *American Fiction in the Cold War*. Madison: U of Wisconsin P, 1991.

Schoene-Harwood, Berthold, ed. *Mary Shelley*: Frankenstein. New York: Columbia UP, 2000.

Schreiber, Evelyn Jaffe. *Subversive Voices: Eroticizing the Other in William Faulkner and Toni Morrison*. Knoxville: U of Tennessee P, 2001.

Schwab, Gabriele. "'If Only I Were Not Obliged to Manifest': Iser's Aesthetics of Negativity." *New Literary History* 31.1 (Winter 2000): 73–89.

Schwartz, Lawrence H. *Creating Faulkner's Reputation: The Politics of Modern Literary Criticism*. Knoxville: U of Tennessee P, 1988.

———. "Toni Morrison and William Faulkner: The Necessity of a Great American Novelist." *Cultural Logic: An Electronic Journal of Marxist Theory and Practice*. 2002 <http://eserver.org/clogic>. April 10, 2005.

Schweickart, Patrocinio P. "Reading Ourselves: Toward a Feminist Theory of Reading." *Gender and Reading: Essays on Readers*. Ed. Elizabeth A. Flynn and Patrocinio P. Schweickart. Baltimore: Johns Hopkins UP, 1986. 31–62.

Scott, Sir Walter. "Remarks on *Frankenstein, or the Modern Prometheus*; A Novel." *Blackwood's Edinburgh Magazine* 2 (20 March–1 April 1818): 613–620.

Scruggs, Charles W. "The City Without Maps in Richard Wright's Native Son." *Critical essays on Richard Wright's* Native Son. Ed. Keneth Kinnamon. New York: Hall, 1997. 147–79.

Shaw, Debra Benita. *Women, Science and Fiction: The Frankenstein Inheritance.* New York: Palgrave, 2000.

Shelley, Mary Wollstonecraft. *Frankenstein, or the Modern Prometheus.* New York: Bantam, 1981.

Shuker-Haines, Timothy, and Umphrey, Martha M. "Gender (De)Mystified: Resistance and Recuperation in Hard-Boiled Female Detective Fiction." *The Detective in American Fiction, Film, and Television.* Ed. Jerome H. Delamater and Ruth Prigozy. Westport, CT: Greenwood, 1998. 71–84.

Shumway, David. *Creating American Civilization: A Genealogy of American Literature as an Academic Discipline.* Minneapolis: U of Minnesota P, 1994.

———. "The Star System in Literary Studies." *PMLA*, 1997 Jan, 112:1, 85–100.

———. "The Star System Revisited." *The Minnesota Review*, 52–54: 175–84.

Siegel, Paul N. "The Conclusion of Richard Wright's *Native Son.*" *Critical Essays on Richard Wright's* Native Son. Ed.Keneth Kinnamon. New York: Hall, 1997. 94–103.

Sinfield, Alan. *Literature, Politics, and Culture in Postwar Britain.* Berkeley: U of California P, 1989.

Siskin, Clifford. "Jane Austen and the Engendering of Disciplinarity." *Jane Austen and Discourses of Feminism.* Ed. Devoney Looser. New York: St. Martin's Press, 1995. 51–67.

Skerrett, Joseph T., Jr. "Composing Bigger: Wright and the Making of *Native Son.*" *Richard Wright: A Collection of Critical Essays.* Ed. Arnold Rampersad. Englewood Cliffs, NJ: Prentice, 1995. 26–39.

Smith, Barbara. "Toward a Black Feminist Criticism." *Feminist Literary Theory: A Reader.* Ed. Mary Eagleton. Oxford: Blackwell, 1996. 122–26.

Smith, Barbara Herrnstein. "Contingencies of Value." Rpt in *The Critical Tradition: Classic Texts and Contemporary Trends.* Ed. David H. Richter. Boston: Bedford, 1998: 1320–44.

Smith, Erin A. *Hard-Boiled: Working-Class Readers and Pulp Magazines.* Philadelphia: Temple UP, 2000.

———. "'Both a Woman and a Complete Professional': Women Readers and Women's Hard-Boiled Detective Fiction." *Reading Sites: Social Difference and Reader Response.* Ed. Patrocinio P. Schweikart and Elizabeth A. Flynn. New York: Modern Language Association of America, 2004. 189–220.

Smith, Henry Nash. "A Sound Heart and a Deformed Conscience." *The Critical Response to Mark Twain's* Huckleberry Finn. Ed. Laurie Champion. Westport, CT: Greenwood Press, 1991. 61–78.

Snow, C. P. *The Two Cultures: And a Second Look*. New York: Mentor Books, 1964.

Southam, B. C., ed. *Jane Austen*: Northanger Abbey and Persuasion *A Casebook*. London: MacMillan, 1976.

————. *Jane Austen: The Critical Heritage*. 2 vols. New York: Routledge & Kegan Paul, 1987.

Spanos, William V. *Repetitions: The Postmodern Occasion in Literature and Culture*. Baton Rouge: Louisiana State University Press, 1987.

Spillane, Mickey. *One Lonely Night*. New York: New American Library, 1951.

————. *The Girl Hunters*. New York: New American Library, 1962.

Spivak, Gayatri Chakravorty. "Three Women's Texts and a Critique of Imperialism." *Critical Inquiry*. 12.1 (Autumn 1985): 243–61.

Staiger, Janet. *Media Reception Studies*. New York: New York UP, 2005.

Stepto, Robert B. "I Thought I Knew These People: Wright and the Afro-American Literary Tradition." *Richard Wright*. Ed. Harold Bloom. New York: Chelsea House, 1987. 57–74.

————. *From Behind the Veil: A Study of Afro-American Narrative*. Urbana: U of Illinois P, 1979.

Sundquist, Eric J. *Faulkner: The House Divided*. Baltimore: Johns Hopkins UP, 1983

Sutherland, John. *How to Read A Novel: A User's Guide*. New York: St. Martin's Press, 2006.

Tally, Justine. *The Story of* Jazz: *Toni Morrison's Dialogic Imagination*. Hamburg: LIT, 2001

Tani, Stefano. *The Doomed Detective: The Contribution of the Detective Novel to Postmodern American and Italian Fiction*. Carbondale: Southern Illinois University Press, 1984.

Taylor, Gary. *Reinventing Shakespeare: A Cultural History from the Restoration to the Present*. New York: Oxford UP, 1989.

Tebbel, John. *Between Covers: The Rise and Transformation of Book Publishing in America*. New York: Oxford UP, 1987.

Tennenhouse, Leonard. *Power on Display: The politics of Shakespeare's genres*. London: Methuen: 1986.

Thomas, Brook. "Restaging the Reception of Iser's Earlier Work, or Sides Not Taken in Discussions of the Aesthetic." *New Literary History* 31.1 (2000): 13–44.

Tompkins, Jane P. *Sensational Designs: The Cultural Work of American Fiction 1790–1860*. New York: Oxford UP, 1985.

Trilling, Lionel. *Sincerity and Authenticity*. Cambridge, MA: Harvard UP, 1972.

———. *The Liberal Imagination: Essays on Literature and Society*. Garden City, NY: Doubleday, 1953.

Turner, Darwin T. *In a Minor Chord: Three Afro-American Writers and Their Search for Identity*. Carbondale: Southern Illinois UP, 1971.

Twain, Mark. *The Adventures of Huckleberry Finn*. New York: Penguin, 1966.

Urkowitz, Steven. "Back to Basics: Thinking about the *Hamlet* First Quarto." *The Hamlet First Published (Q1, 1603) Origins, Form, Intertextualities*. Ed. by Thomas Clayton. Newark: University of Delaware Press, 1992: 257–91.

Vanacker, Sabine. "V.I. Warshawski, Kinsey Millhone and Kay Scarpetta: Creating a Feminist Detective Hero." *Criminal Proceedings: The Contemporary American Crime Novel*. London: Pluto Press, 1997. 62–86

Vaquin, Monette. Frankenstein *ou les délires de la raison*. Paris: Éditions François Bourin, 1989.

Veeder, William. *Mary Shelley and* Frankenstein, *the Fate of Androgyny*. Chicago: U of Chicago P, 1986.

Vickery, Olga. *The Novels of William Faulkner*. Baton Rouge: Louisiana State UP, 1959.

Waggoner, Hyatt H. *William Faulkner: From Jefferson to the World*. Lexington: U of Kentucky P. 1959

Wallace, Michele. *Black Macho and the Myth of Superwoman*. London: Verso, 1980.

———. "Negative images: towards a black feminist cultural criticism." *The Cultural Studies Reader*. Ed. Simon During. London: Routledge,1993. 118–31.

Walton, Priscilla L., and Jones, Manina. *Detective Agency: Women Rewriting the Hard-Boiled Tradition*. Los Angeles: U of California P, 1999.

Warren, Robert Penn. "William Faulkner." *William Faulkner: Three Decades of Criticism*. Ed. Frederick J. Hoffman and Olga W. Vickery. New York: Harcourt, Brace, Jovanovich, 1960. 109–24.

Washington, Mary Helen. "Foreward." *Their Eyes Were Watching God*. New York: Harper & Row, 1990. vii-xiv.

Weinstein, Philip M. *What Else But Love? The Ordeal of Race in Faulkner and Morrison*. New York: Columbia UP, 1996.

Wellek, René. *A History of Modern Criticism: 1750–1950*. New Haven, CT: Yale UP, 1965. 5 vols.

Wenning, Mario. "Heidegger and Adorno: Opening up Grounds for Dialogue." *Gnosis* Volume 6.1 (2002). July 12, 2004. <http://artsandscience.concordia.ca/philosophy/gnosis/vol_vi/index.html#toc>

Werner, Craig. "Bigger's Blues: *Native Son* and the Articulation of Afro-American Modernism." *New Essays on* Native Son. Ed. Keneth Kinnamon. Cambridge: Cambridge UP, 1990. 117–52.

West, Cornell. *Keeping Faith: Philosophy and Race in America.* New York: Routledge, 1993.

Whately, Richard. *Quarterly Review* 24 (January 1821). Cited in *Jane Austen*: Northanger Abbey and Persuasion *A Casebook.* Ed. B. C. Southam. London: MacMillan, 1976. 50–51.

White, Hayden. *Tropics of Discourse: Essays in Cultural Criticism.* Baltimore: Johns Hopkins UP, 1978.

Widdowson, Peter. *Hardy in History: A Study in Literary Sociology.* London: Routledge, 1989.

Wiegman, Robyn. "Difference and Disciplinarity." *Aesthetics in a Multicultural Age.* Ed. Emory Elliott, Louis Freitas, and Jeffrey Rhyne. New York: Oxford UP, 2002. 135–56.

Williams, Jeffrey. "Name Recognition." *The Minnesota Review,* 52–54: 185–208.

———. "The Posttheory Generation." *Symploke,* 3, 1 (Winter 1995): 55–76.

Williams, Raymond. *The Long Revolution.* New York: Columbia UP, 1961.

Wilson, Ann. "The Female Dick and the Crisis of Heterosexuality." *Feminism in Women's Detective Fiction.* Ed. Glenwood Irons. Toronto: Toronto UP, 1995. 148–56.

Wilt, Judith. *Ghosts of the Gothic: Austen, Eliot, & Lawrence.* Princeton, NJ: Princeton UP, 1980.

Wittenberg, Judith Bryant. "Race in *Light in August*: Wordsymbols and Obverse Reflections." *The Cambridge Companion to William Faulkner.* Ed. Philip M. Weinstein. Cambridge: Cambridge UP, 1995 146–167.

Wolfson, Susan J., ed. *Frankenstein; or the Modern Prometheus.* New York: Longman, 2003.

Woodard, Fredrick and Donnarae MacCann. "Minstrel Shackles and Nineteenth-Century 'Liberality' in *Huckleberry Finn.*" *Satire or Evasion? Black Perspectives on* Huckleberry Finn. Ed. James S. Leonard, Thomas A. Tenney, and Thadious M. Davis. Durham, NC: Duke UP, 1992. 141–53.

Woof, R. S. Review of *The Diaries and Correspondence of James Losh. Notes and Queries* 21 (November 1965), 433–436. Cited in Lyles, W. H. *Mary Shelley: An Annotated Bibliography.* New York: Garland, 1975. 166.

Wordsworth, William. "Preface to *Lyrical Ballads.*" *The Critical Tradition: Classical Texts and Contemporary Trends.* Ed. David H. Richter. New York: St. Martin's, 1989. 285–98.

Wright, Richard. "Between Laughter and Tears." *Zora Neale Hurston: Critical Perspectives Past and Present*. Ed. K. A. Appiah and Henry Louis Gates Jr. New York: Amistad, 1993. 16–17.

———. *Native Son*. New York: HarperCollins, 1989.

Ziarek, Ewa Plonowska. "Mimesis in Black and White: Feminist Aesthetics, Negativity and Semblance." *The New Aestheticism*. Eds. John J. Joughin and Simon Malpas. Manchester: Manchester UP, 2003. 51–67.

Ziarek, Krzysztof. *Radical Art: Reflections after Adorno and Heidegger. Adorno: A Critical Reader*. Ed. Nigel Gibson and Andrew Rubin. Malden, MA: Blackwell; 2002: 341–60.

Žižek, Slavoj. "The Lesson of Rancière." *The Politics of Aesthetics: The Distribution of the Sensible*. Trans. and intro. Gabriel Rockhill. London: Continuum, 2004. 69–79.